PRISONS I HAVE
(An Unexpected Li

By Harry Crew

Edited by Alison Dempster

Introduction by Brian Lewis

Design: John Young

Published by Eebygumbooks

www.eebygumbooks.co.uk

Distributed by Amazon

©Harry Crew 2017

Front Cover: *This wall hanging depicting "TIME" was made by women prisoners in the Education Department of Askham Grange Prison and given to me on my retirement in 2000. I love it and it hangs on my bedroom wall.*

For Sarah, Anthony and Martyn

I keep six honest serving-men
(They taught me all I knew);
Their names are What and Why and When
And How and Where and Who. (Kipling)

And for my Ex, Helen, who supported me
during my prison years

Contents

Inside the Insider Inside

Introduction: Brian Lewis

Foreword: Harry Crew

1 **Beginnings**

2 **Borstal After-Care and Beyond**

3 **Initiation**

4 **Prison Apprenticeship 1**

5 **Prison Apprenticeship 2**

6 **Askham Grange Prison for Women**

7 **The Barking Mad Governor: Experiences with the Press**

8 **Reflections**

   Acknowledgments

   Appendices

   Family Documents

Inside the Insider, Inside

"It is so difficult to put into words all the emotions one feels during a prison sentence.

DESPAIR of being away from the ones you love, partners, children, husbands, family and friends.

CONFUSION of being away from home and not having familiar things of your own around you.

TRAUMA of living in close confinement with people with whom you have nothing in common, and who may well have very different standards from your own.

MISERY of having no control over your own life and all decisions being made for you.

ADJUSTING to a life that is alien to what you are used to, particularly if you have been used to a position of authority or worked in a profession.

LOSS of individuality, you become a non-person; a number, you feel that you have lost your personality. You have lost your job, your professional qualifications, your home, pets, some friends and family, because of going to prison.

DIGNITY is taken from you, the humiliation of strip searches, of being mistrusted by staff and of being "talked down" to.

STRESS of not being able to deal with the problems that arise at home and become more complicated because of being in prison.

TENSION of never being alone even to have a cry when you feel the need to.

HOPELESSNESS of having to cope in such conditions for a long time can well bring on stress related illness, sleeplessness and apathy.

CONFIDENCE is lost, you wonder if it can ever be regained, and whether you will ever be able to pick up the threads of your life again.

PRESSURE of the constant noise, it is so destructive you can never seem to get away from it. People shouting, swearing, feet clomping, everybody seems to wear heavy boots, doors banging, radios and TV blaring, all so very difficult to deal with if you are a quiet, private person.

PAIN of the hurt and shame you have brought on those who love you. And it is going to be with you, maybe for ever.

COST I think it is true to say that only rich people should be sent to prison. The cost of buying the things needed to make life a little more bearable, e.g. toiletries, coffee, tea, stamps and phone cards are very important.

The biggest cost of all is the visits to the prison, or the open visit. Askham is very difficult to reach, due to its situation; the bus service is poor and taxis are very expensive. It may well be a long way away, and some people are unable to visit because of the cost, which in turn puts extra pressure on a relationship which is already stressed.

Although I did not personally have a prison visitor, some of my friends did, and I got to know some of them well. I can only say Thank God that there are such people, who are prepared to give up their time to visit people, who would otherwise never have a visit.

It means so much to be able to talk to someone outside the prison service. Someone they can trust to keep a confidence, and who talks to you as though you are a human being. This means so very much to your self esteem.

Not all experiences in prison are totally negative, there are a couple of positive ones, mainly the friendships that can be made, that will survive after a prison sentence is over. There are courses available, and it is possible to gain some qualifications, maybe for some, the only ones they will ever obtain. It is possible to discover talents that you never knew you possessed, perhaps time to reflect, and get to know yourself.

To conclude, I really feel that prison does not achieve enough positive things. Lives, relationships, careers, homes and families are destroyed by it. I am sure there are much better alternatives that should be considered for a great number of the people who are sent to prison. Of course, obviously there are some people who have to be put there because they are a danger to the public, but they should also get the help that they require during their sentence.

Weekend prison must be considered as an option, to enable jobs to be kept, relationships to survive, families to stay together and homes to be maintained. More use of community work and electronic tagging must be a step in the right direction, and the people who need medical and psychiatric care should get that, rather than a prison sentence. Much more should be done to help the people dependent on drugs or alcohol, and advice should be given to those needing financial help. All these things are required to enable people to go on and do something useful with their lives.

This is the opinion of the Insider inside:

"However well deserved, prison damages the individual, as indicated here. Sometimes the passage of time or the learning gained can mitigate the experience; the real and many challenges come after release. The "Insider" here, a mature, educated woman, took her own life shortly after her return home."

Introduction

In 1996 I spoke at a meeting on board a boat called *Sobriety*, which was moored on Goole Quays. In the talk I explained that, amongst a range of programmes the Yorkshire Arts Charity (an educational charity with a fifteen year record) had devised was one that enabled communities to recognize their value by publishing books about their achievements. I called it a "Book in a Day experiment". When the meeting was over, I was approached by a man in his mid-fifties, Harry Crew, who introduced himself as the Governor of an open prison for women. His prison, Askham Grange (near York), had supplied women for some time to assist in crewing the boat, explaining that prisoners were allowed out as part of their resettlement towards eventual release. Prisoners deemed suitable and trustworthy worked in various employments and charities or attended Higher Education College courses in York and Askham Bryan Agricultural College.

He didn't spend much time on small talk but came straight to the point. "Do you think you could do a Book in a Day about a prison, and would it interest you?" I did not hesitate but replied that I thought we could. We fixed a date to explore the idea further. Up to that point my experience of prison and institutional life in general was limited. I had worked for a short time in Wakefield Prison, and as a young man, in what was called in those days a "Mental Home", but my career up to age forty had been in education. I had worked with older "special needs" children and developed courses in deprived areas so I was not without knowledge of related areas of work, so the challenge to develop the idea of a book involving interaction with prisoners and staff at Askham was enticing.

A week or two later I found myself outside the gates of what had once been a nineteenth century gentleman's residence about five miles from the centre of York. Situated in pleasant, well-tended ornamental grounds, it struck me that this was a place that aimed to reform, not to punish. I was not disappointed, but it quickly became apparent that any book would take more than a day to write, for it meant gaining the trust of staff and satisfying the curiosity of prisoners. I was given the freedom to explore and to walk and talk to anyone and everyone, with Harry filling in background history and providing insights into prison practice and culture. I enjoyed the experience and am pleased that the end result culminated in the award-winning book, "Askham: The Story of a House".

As I came to know him I saw that Harry and I had things in common. We left school, neither of us having done particularly well, and made the most of unexpected opportunities. We were from caring, working-class families, he in London and me in Birmingham. We took chances and made the best of them – both of us unconventional – me in education, he in prison. We were pragmatists with a good dash of idealism, who tended to move instinctively, with end products appearing in forms that surprised us, and cemented the friendship. Eventually I persuaded him to write "Prisons I Have Known", for he has a valuable story about his career in a variety of prison institutions, especially, as he says, the "most difficult and satisfying culmination as Governor of a prison for women", giving us an insight into prison life, rarely written about.

Brian Lewis

Foreword

The Governor said: "Sit down Crew. When I say "Jump!" every fucker jumps, and that includes you." Somewhat shaken I wondered just what I had let myself in for; it was certainly a colourful introduction to my first posting where I was to spend the next three years. This book although in part family history primarily tells of my experiences from fairly humble beginnings to a career which eventually led me to govern a small Yorkshire prison for women. It is based on notes written for my children to give a flavour of what I was up to whilst they were growing up, but it has been at the encouragement of Brian Lewis, author and artist, who suggested that I write more fully an account which might be of some interest. I would stress that it has not been my intent to produce an academic tome on penal matters and it is written some sixteen years after my retirement and as such comes from memories which, as we tend to do, favour the happy ones and forget much of the bad. I hope the reader finds some instances which might bring to mind the TV series "Porridge".

I have taken the liberty to copy the title of my book from one written some seventy years ago by Mary Size the first Governor of H M Prison Askham Grange, for it was from her account I gained much insight into the running of an open prison for women.

Harry Crew

Me at gate of HM Prison Askham Grange

1. Beginnings

From as far back as 1747 it has been possible to establish that my forebears on my father's side were watermen on the River Thames who, having served their apprenticeship of seven years, were entitled to be called "Freemen of the River". They belonged to The Company of Watermen (later Watermen and Lightermen), one of the City of London guilds. Effectively they were the waterborne taxi service and like London taxi drivers today, who are required to have extensive knowledge of the roads, they had then to have full knowledge of the geography and tides of the river and would have plied their trade of conveying customers and goods along or across the river, or taking people to and from the many ships that frequented the port of London. Apparently they were renowned for earthy and foul language and not unknown to accept a fare, row into mid-stream and then demand extra payment!

As sail gave way to steam, and traffic on the river moved away from the oarsman with his ferryboat, my grandfather gave up the river work and became a porter at Billingsgate Fish Market, where he worked until he was in his seventies. He and his wife had seven children: two girls and five boys. My father, born in 1910, was the fourth youngest boy and caught Polio as a child which left him with a "gammy" leg requiring a boot with leg irons for support. Of course there was no Health Service and it is evident from the costed receipts that it was a struggle to provide for this disability as his feet grew. My father on leaving school showed his determination to get work but of course his disability restricted what he could do, and the economic depression of the 1930s did not help. In 1930 he purchased a box-trike and set up as a mobile seller of sweets; later in 1933 he had his own wet fish stall, receiving his fish fresh from Billingsgate courtesy of his father and older brother, both porters there. This he discontinued on the outbreak of WWII when he had to register for military service.

My father and mother married in 1937. My mother's father had worked on the railways as a steam engine driver. He died in 1947 and I remember very little of him. Mother had a sister, and whilst single, both were enthusiastic members of the Baptist church, in fact helping to found a church in Bellingham, near Catford in south London.

I was born in Guy's Hospital – just within the sound of Bow Bells - which makes me a "Cockney" - in July 1940, a year after war had been declared and a day or two before the Battle of Britain. My parents had had the disappointment of a stillborn baby girl before I arrived, and my brother David was born two years after me. Both of us had to be delivered by caesarean section, which was not pleasant for my mother given the state of things, the war being in process and before the days of the National Health Service. It was apparent that we two boys were to be the extent of the family as my father let slip "mum has shut up shop"!

I do not remember being bombed out of our home in Bermondsey, South London, nor the move into temporary accommodation before we re-located to what was to become our permanent home in Revelon Road, Brockley. I do have memories of having a gas mask and being taken down into our cellar during air raids. The air raid siren was a haunting sound and ever after, my mother could not bear to hear it if played on the TV or radio. Towards the end of the war I have two particular memories; being taken for a ride in my uncle Len's jeep (he being a member of a bomb disposal squad) and also, whilst sitting at a meal, suddenly finding myself under the table; my chair and the surrounding area covered with ceiling plaster which had fallen down as the result of a V2 rocket exploding further along the street. I don't know if anyone was killed, but the resulting bombsite provided hours of exploration and occupation for us street children over the next few years. The site, which covered an area of several houses between two parallel roads, remained debris strewn from the demolished houses for several years and our infant street gangs often had brick fights, which apart from the occasional cuts and abrasions (amazingly, with hindsight) gave rise to no serious injury.

Early in the war I was evacuated with my mother, but as my father remained in London my mother soon decided that she would return to be with him, the view being taken that if we died we would do so together. Due to his childhood polio disability my father was registered unfit for war service, but did his bit as a telephonist at Vauxhall gas works, which was a target in the London air raids and a pretty dangerous place to be, especially as he had to travel the five or six miles each way by bicycle, often through bomb damaged streets.

I have three memories which stand out for me in the immediate aftermath of the war. The first is being taken by my father into the centre of London, to my first trip on the Underground. This was for either VE or VJ day, when everyone was celebrating the final end to the war. Whilst on the train I recited a verse taught me by my father and this amused an American soldier, who pressed five shillings into my hand - my first earnings.

" 'right behind, 'right in front
 Now we're off with a puff and a grunt
 "Tickets Please" No delays
 Slam the doors and right away."

A second memory is going to stay at Aldenham, then a sleepy country village in Hertfordshire where my father's sister and her husband lived. She had been in the Land Army during the war and had worked on the farm where he was foreman. Whilst staying there I was playing in the garden when a large formation of bomber type aircraft flew overhead - I ran screaming into the house to be reassured that "they were ours" and therefore not a danger. I would have been in my fifth or sixth year, and it shows how conditioned to air raids I had become.

The third is rationing. This was imposed during WWII when each family was allocated a ration book of coupons for all essential items including clothing, meat and, especially where we children were concerned, sweets. Having been born into this, we knew no different. Also a complete lack of some fruit; for instance I was completely thrown at age six by my first banana, not knowing that it had to have the skin peeled back!

After the end of the war my father was replaced at the gas works and took a government training course as a boot and shoemaker/repairer. As a result our shoes were always repaired at home with leather and iron tips, the upside being that they lasted a long time, the downside that they weighed a ton. I can still conjure up the sight and smell of leather soaking for some days before being deemed pliable enough to work. A one-off event entailed the making of a fish porter's flat-topped leather hat for my uncle. A plaster cast was made of his head, leather was soaked and duly the hat took shape having been sewn, riveted and heavily waxed. The flat top was to aid the balancing of boxes of fish carried on the head, and a large upturned brim surrounded the hat to catch the wet slime that dripped from the boxes.

We had gas lighting in the house until 1947, when electricity was installed. There was no bathroom and this was solved by a large tin bath being brought into the kitchen from the garden, and filled with hot water from saucepans heated on the gas stove. We then all went in sequence into the tub, refilling with hot water - the majority of the previous dirty water remaining in the bath.

There was an indoor WC but my father thought this was for emergency only, and that it was healthier to use the outside lavatory - come rain, snow and all weather - note that soft toilet paper did not exist and it was either newspaper squares or, if lucky, the thick shiny one sided proprietary brand, both of which could leave one with a sore bottom. My father cut our hair, and hair being caught in the manual clippers was ever a dreaded experience.

At some point, dad worked as a lift operator in a government building. He then worked from home, making metal flower holders, sold to fit into vases. This was piecework employment, which was extremely cruel to his hands, for it meant bending strips of heavy-gauge wire to create the type of holder required. He then gained in 1951 his longest period of employment at the Royal Victualling Yard, Deptford, where he worked for some 12 years before discharge on medical grounds. Thereafter he had a succession of short term jobs; the spirit was willing, but his health was failing. As a result, my mother went to work part time as a typist. With my brother and I at grammar school our parents' financial situation was always precarious. Thankfully there were one or two charities that helped with grants, for there was little state aid. Through one of these, the Edridge Fund, I was later to receive from its volunteer Secretary the offer of a job that led me later into a career in prison. We also had a lodger in the late 1940s who came originally from Waterford in Ireland and had spent his life in the Royal Navy. He was a quiet but fascinating man who had gone to sea in the age of steam, had his ship sunk under him in the First World War and again in the second.

Although my mother was a Baptist, my father believed deeds mattered more than words and therefore remained a sceptic of excessive religiosity. To please her we all went to her church where my brother and I found the sermons interminable, lasting as they did upwards of an hour. I think my father enjoyed the singing most, for he had a fine baritone voice. At Christmas when we walked the five miles to my grandparents' home in Bermondsey, where all the family gathered, my father would challenge us children to suggest a word or subject, whereupon he would sing a song from his extensive repertoire. Needless to say, we tried to suggest something to beat him but he always managed to make some connection. He would also do monologues such as "The green eye of the little yellow god" by Milton Hayes or "The shooting of Dan McGrew" and others by Robert Service, with music provided by my aunt, and we children providing "noises off". There was, of course, no television, and entertainment was self-made.

Dad was a man of high principle and strong views. He firmly believed that a liar was worse than a thief because a thief could (only) steal your money, but a liar could steal your good name. He had a great sense of humour and when in the mood we would get him laughing until tears ran down his face. Also a man of compassion - I remember a new neighbour coming to ask if he could borrow ten shillings for a few days, my father lent it to him and when I asked him why (because I was aware of our own shortage of money), he replied that it was worth taking the risk to find out whether the man was of reputable character. He would always tell us to ask the question "Why?" because although it might get us into trouble sometimes, it was always better to challenge rather than accept simply what we were told, without thinking it through. I remember him recounting that whilst away from home he ran out of petrol for the invalid car he had been allocated and a passing motorist had taken the trouble to fetch him some. When Dad had wanted to pay for the petrol the motorist had refused, simply saying: "Put it in the pot". When dad showed some puzzlement, the motorist explained that when Dad saw someone needing assistance, his help would be the payback. My father was impressed enough to recount this to us boys and thereby encouraged our faith in human nature.

It was usual at the time to start school at age five, as there were no playgroups etc., and to me it was a shock. I remember having to be pushed through the gates and a few tears being shed. We all sat in rows at desks and had to keep quiet, learning by rote with break time as the only opportunity to let off steam - once I fell in the playground and cut the bridge of my nose (a scar I carry still). I was very slow learning to read and had great difficulty, until a teacher, Miss Gutteridge, to whom I was ever after grateful, gave me a copy of *Black Beauty* to try - I loved it. Once started, there was no stopping me, and I became a real bookworm. I left Mantle Road Infant School at the age of seven, transferring to Turnham Road Junior School where I proved to be a plodder. As we all did, I sat the 11 plus exam and, I suspect, primarily on the recommendation of the Headmaster I passed for Grammar School. I remember him visiting our house to satisfy himself that my father would find the extra expense involved. Whilst the education was free, there was a formidable list of school clothing including sports-wear - and he knew that we boys often had free school dinners due to my father's periods of sickness and his difficulties in sustaining employment.

In 1951 I went to Brockley County Grammar School on Hilly Fields, Ladywell, South East London. This was some two miles from my home and I initially walked both ways on my own or with friends; later I cycled. Few in our locality had cars so it was normal to walk or take public transport, which meant the train or tram; later the bus replaced the tram and steam trains were phased out. The school, boys only, was located in a park land setting, which was an ideal location, allowing us great freedom during lunch periods. I was not a bright student, having to work hard at homework for anything to sink in and I was also shy and somewhat introverted which led to some bullying. The need for effort to get anything to stick grieved me because other lads seemed to be able to absorb facts and regurgitate them in exams without difficulty. I found exams difficult because I was often unsure as to the specifics of the question - apparently I over-complicated issues, and ended up dithering. I did tolerably well at Geography and History, both of which caught my imagination, in Maths and English Language I coped but in foreign languages and science I was none too good. In fact at the end of, understandably, my only year of Latin I disgraced myself by coming bottom of the class with just five per cent in the exam, so that ended my classical education! I took my GCE in 1956 at sixteen years of age, but only passed in two subjects. My parents permitted me to return into the 5th Remove - in other words a class for those who had not gained the number of passes expected, and I subsequently gained a further two passes. In those days there were no grades, you either passed or you didn't.

My main preoccupation was flying, which was available to us through membership of the school Air Training Corps squadron. These were the days of the piston engine aircraft and I undertook my first flight in an Anson, the most significant memory is of the way the wings flexed up and down like an ungainly goose. The Chipmunk RAF trainer was enjoyable, though the pilots tried by aerobatics to make us cadets sick, which meant that we would have to clear up the cockpit (if we didn't get it all into the strong paper bag supplied), enabling the pilot to go for a cup of tea. I was never sick, although it was often a close call. On one occasion a cockpit window blew out and whilst the pilot calmly told me not to worry, he nevertheless reminded me of parachute deployment - although I think this was simply RAF humour.

The most unusual flight was in a Short Sunderland flying boat during an annual summer camp. We spent idyllic hours cruising up and down the flight path in an RAF motorboat, making sure that there was no debris in the water until our turn for a flight came. This was quite eventful, for the aircraft had, as far as I recall, no door, or it was fixed in the open position, and whilst an aircrew member was pointing out a landmark he failed to hear the warning klaxon and the aircraft banked - we nearly lost a cadet and an airman through the doorway. Another time, I was taken up in one of the last Lincoln heavy bombers (a development of the Lancaster of WWII fame) and was told after take-off that I might go into the Plexiglas nose where the bomb aimer would be located when releasing the bombs. I remember being there for some hours, just cruising up and down the North Sea, during which I could see the pilots keeping themselves occupied with cheap novelettes of the Hank Jansen variety whilst the plane flew on autopilot. When we came into land I was still in the nose and enjoyed seeing the ground rushing up to meet us, however the pilot (when he remembered my presence after we had landed), obviously realized that he had made a bad error, allowing me to remain in what was potentially a very dangerous place.

I was also a member of the squadron shooting team, gaining my marksman badge, and regularly took my .22 or .303 rifle home - minus the firing mechanism. We had a small .22 firing range on the roof of the school and we were allowed to practice there - some cadets, (not me for I hadn't the "dare element") - would fire off at the park keepers, but I cannot recall any complaints by anyone having been hit. It taught me a lasting respect for guns. The discipline of parades, smartness and responding to orders was accepted and, on looking back, stood me well throughout my life. In my last years at school I expected to be called up for compulsory National Service at 18 years, and had been thinking about the RAF as a career, however just before I left school this was ended and I was at a loss as to what to do. In truth I knew more about what I did not want, i.e. banking or insurance, as suggested by the careers teacher. My father had probably mentioned this to the volunteer visitor from the Edridge Fund during one of their meetings, for about the time I left school I was offered and, for want of something else to do, accepted the "office boy" position at Borstal After-Care, a division of the Central After-Care Association. This was to set me off into my career "in crime".

My teens coincided with the rock and roll years of the mid 1950s through into the "swinging sixties". I cannot recall exactly how I became a member of the local church youth group but our group of about twelve to fifteen at most was a loose collection of those aged thirteen to sixteen. In different and changing subgroups we went everywhere together, thinking nothing of walking the six miles into central London for an evening - and back afterwards. We would go to Chatham Navy days when it was possible to clamber over naval ships, rambles in the country and house parties as well as any ad hoc adventure that might appeal. On reflection, the thread which held us together was the youth club evening, and the fact that most of us attended evensong on a Sunday night after which we either hung around the street corner chatting, or went on to someone's house where we were usually allowed use of the "front room". I lived on my bike and cycled for miles around south London and the outer suburbs of Bromley, Hayes and Sevenoaks and into Kent, without thought of danger in any form – except on the one occasion I was hit by a car.

There was also the search for "what's it all about?" Having been brought up with some religious background, I rebelled against the strictures of my mother's' practice yet I was influenced by my father's humanitarianism; I was also a member of a Church of England youth club, so Ken Dobson, the local curate, was a good start. He devoted hours to our questions and, often on our part, heated arguments and a few of us visited other denominations' places of worship. It should not be construed that we were so intense as to the exclusion of normal teen activities although I did read the bible cover to cover, leaving out the "begets" and other seemingly repetitious bits. Eventually I accepted the tenets of the Church of England. The verses which impacted on me were Matthew 25 vs 35-40, as did the poem "Abou Ben Adhem", by Leigh Hunt. However the curate knew us well for he said the church was likely to lose us whilst we were in mid-life, but might well see us back later. I am still not sure where I stand and suppose that I am my father's son, i.e. I feel that deeds take precedence over talk. It seems to me that most faiths wish to promote "good" rather than "evil" behaviour, but it is the curse of arrogance which gets in the way.

As we got older we became fashion-conscious, mostly favouring the "mod" or Italian style dress rather than the "teddy boy". Music started with Bill Haley and the Comets, Elvis Presley, Cliff Richard, The Beatles, The Rolling Stones, and all the rest of the rock and roll stars of the era. Wanting to stretch our wings we started to hope for motorbike and car ownership. I preferred a car, although it took me three attempts to pass my driving test at nineteen, after that I was never without one. Usually I changed my cars at six-month intervals, mostly because they broke down. My first car (a Ford Anglia (1934)) I spent much time pushing, but I persevered because girls expected boys to have a car. Petrol was about 3/6d (15 pence) a gallon.

My brother David and me, 1949

Brother David and me helping on the farm with my uncle John Hume at Aldenham, Herts, c.1952

The family: Mum, David, Dad and me, 1954

Dad's invalid car with David, Mum and Dad, c.1957

Me as office boy

Borstal Aftercare staff who introduced me (bottom front) to a career in crime

2. Borstal After-Care and Beyond

I started at Borstal After-Care as the office boy in 1957 at a salary of £4.12 shillings per week, with the promise that my pay would increase when I had learned to type. This I quickly did, using two fingers. My first experience of "inside" was to go with some colleagues to Feltham Borstal, where we saw the staff and Borstal lads putting on a performance of the Terence Rattigan play *The Winslow Boy*. In subsequent years I visited Huntercombe Borstal for the annual Borstal After-Care vs staff and lads' cricket match. This was when Sir Almeric Rich was governor, and I was intrigued when I learnt that he often did any punishment alongside the lad to whom he had given an award, e.g. if it was extra cleaning duties he would clean alongside the youth, thus demonstrating his own awareness of the task which he had imposed, and his preparedness to do the punishment he had ordered. The whole subject of the development of the Borstal System and the treatment of young offenders began to interest me. People like Evelyn Ruggles-Brise and Alexander Paterson inspired me and I read many books on people's prison experience – prisoners, staff and academics alike. I also began evening classes studying Psychology and Sociology.

Whilst working in a clerical (now "administrative") environment, I absorbed the ethos of what had started as, and still remained, despite government funding, a voluntary independent organisation. The Borstal Association was set-up to arrange for the supervision of young men discharged from a Borstal Institution. 1908 saw the introduction of the Borstal System, whereby young offenders (i.e. those under twenty-one years of age) would be treated as a separate category from the adult penal system. There were trials at Bedford and Portland prisons, trying to give a more constructive approach to the treatment of young people, but the use of the prison at

Borstal near Rochester in Kent was to give its name to a completely new system of dealing with young men in custody. The sentence was to be spent part in the institution and the balance under controlled supervision in society. The Borstal Trainee had to serve a minimum of nine months and not more than three years "inside", and then had to demonstrate by his efforts and progress that he could be discharged. The whole duration was four years in total. Usually Probation Officers acted as our "Associates" in the field but there were still a few voluntary bodies involved, e.g. The St Vincent de Paul Society in Ireland. However "after-care" was not a core piece of work and much depended upon the Probation Officer's own interest as to how much priority he gave it. The Probation Service had evolved from the Police Court Missionaries of old and had the purpose of "Advise, Assist and Befriend"; the same ethos pervaded the Borstal Association, although this is not to say that any trainee failing to keep to the terms of his Supervision Order would not be speedily recalled to serve a further six months at Portsmouth or Reading Recall Centre. Such action was by executive order of the Prison Commission based on our report, and there being no requirement for a court hearing since the lad was simply being returned to serve a sentence which had already been passed.

I was taught early and emphatically that when one handled a lad's file one was handling his life – a lesson which should be mandatory for all who make decisions by reading people's files. I was also told that any fool could say "Yes", it was much harder to say "No", and that it was important and kinder to face up to this when necessary (but that there could often be found a way to soften the impact). Later I was to meet those whose automatic response was "No", given without any consideration whatsoever.

During these years I took training as a Part-time Youth Leader with the London County Council. At the time, leadership was emphasised, as were practical experiences, and therefore I did placements at various youth centres in South London as well as lectures and weekend study groups. It was an intensive two years, whilst holding down my day job. It led to me continuing in a voluntary capacity for many years at the Crossed Swords Youth Centre in Southwark. It was there that for the only time in my life I was assaulted quite badly when I stood in the way of an invading gang and suffered as a consequence. Ever after I was able to say to Prison staff that they were much safer with the availability of backup whilst those working in the community did so often without anyone to come to their aid. It was also there that I learned about group work, seeing the formation of and interaction between groups, which was to become of relevance to me in penal establishments. I later served on the management committee of a youth club in Aylesbury, but it was after my retirement that I returned to community youth work and also did some work with the Youth Justice Service on Referral Orders – but this is jumping ahead.

When eventually promoted I visited Borstals and supervised some lads who were the direct responsibility of the office. On one occasion I visited the Boys Wing at Wormwood Scrubs, when upon arrival I was gaily told by the Gate Officer: "Oh, just go up the side of that wing, turn right (may have been left) and at the door of the wing in front, just knock on the door" – it was somewhat different thirty-odd years later when I went back as part of an inspection team! More senior staff also visited a designated Borstal each month, to interview those trainees shortly to be discharged, to ensure that suitable resettlement plans had been arranged. Many youths stated a wish to move to another area, being afraid to face up to a return to a home town where they were known; this was not usually allowed because experience showed that a youngster in a strange environment was prey to malign influences or exploitation. My responsibility was a monthly visit to Wetherby Borstal in North Yorkshire which was at the time an open establishment (i.e. there was no physical security fence), and it was here that I came to know the Housemasters / Assistant Governors, and gained an understanding of their work. I heard tales of governors who took chances; one let a Borstal lad who married during his sentence stay for his wedding night in his own prison quarter, another let a disabled trainee have his "invalid car" on site and practice driving until he passed his test, and he was then allowed to proceed on home leave in it. There were other acts of significant kindness, all of which made an impression on me, pointing up that rehabilitation could start to take place alongside the punishment which is loss of liberty.

Occasionally I would accompany Peter Smith, one of our full time Supervisors, on his home visits to "learn the trade". I recall his advice when visiting one tenement building near the Elephant and Castle district of South London to always keep to the centre of a passage because the walls might be verminous or just plain filthy - and sometimes one did feel like cleaning one's shoes on departure! Little tips were helpful too, for when he had a suitcase of a lads clothing which required washing, we visited a launderette where Peter played the helpless male, and the female supervisor did the business for him. I would have been about twenty when I was asked to assist with a lad, John, who had left Borstal to live in lodgings arranged for him. Because he lived nearby I occasionally had him home to tea, and took him to the youth club in which I was involved. One evening he arrived at my house, obviously in pain, and on enquiry revealed that he had tooth ache. I took him to an evening dental surgery where his tooth was extracted and he immediately recovered to his usual self. He had, in fact, tried to remove the tooth himself using a pair of pliers and had shattered it, he had done this because he had walked past several dentists but seeing the white-coated receptionist, had lacked the courage to go in. He had been raised in institutions all his life, where every need had been catered for including either a visiting dentist, or someone to accompany him. Because I took him that was all that was necessary to see him through – the lesson for me was to witness the resulting damage of institutionalization. I then began to understand Paterson's dictum, to the effect that you cannot train people for freedom in conditions of captivity.

I married in 1966 and Sarah, our first, was born in 1967. We did her no favour in her name because initial and surname together did not help her at school when I joined the Prison Service. We bought a house for £2250 (!) in Faversham, Kent and it was there Anthony was born in 1969. I left the Borstal Association in 1967 because it was to become absorbed into the Prison Commission (which itself was subsequently absorbed into the Home Office), as a result of the 1963 Advisory Council for the Treatment of Offenders Report which recommended that the Probation Service assume direct control of After-Care and also by this time I wanted to widen my experience and work more directly with people.

At the London Borough of Lewisham in South London I worked as a social worker, mainly with homeless families who were primarily housed in two large tenement blocks, but I also did a spell working with the blind, aged and handicapped. The latter I found very depressing and frustrating work, especially being aware of so many of their problems having had a disabled father myself. My frustration arose out of the huge caseload. Many of the 'clients' had died since they were last visited and also the fact that it took ages for any practical aids recommended to be installed – I supposed that it saved money if the person died in the interim! One experience was to join a party of staff taking some badly disabled young people for a holiday in Paris, where we were something of a curiosity, since it seemed at that time in France most handicapped folk were shut away in institutions. Of particular note was struggling to carry a wheelchair-bound, very overweight youngster up several flights of stairs to see the Mona Lisa, whereupon he grunted that he saw no merit in the painting - after which he was fortunate to be carried down! Otherwise the experience as a whole was a fun-filled time with the youngsters a delight, given their most debilitating handicaps. I greatly admired my colleagues doing this work although they could not understand why I could be interested in people who were anti-social. From having been unsure of what I wanted to do when I left school, I was now certain that it was to be a life working with those who had broken the law.

My time with homeless families was challenging. The majority of the families had been evicted for failing to pay their rent but also a few others who had suffered having been burned out of their homes, or sometimes due to flood damage. It was there whilst doing a "duty" day in the office that I experienced the willingness of mothers to use their children as a bargaining counter to get their own way. Occasionally it was "If you won't give me a flat / change of flat / a house / furniture (or whatever), keep the child(ren)". Our response was that we would have to notify the Children's Department who would take the child into care. This usually caused the mother to snatch the child and leave with a barrage of invective. Having been to a boys' school, only having a brother and working with mostly my own sex, my knowledge of women was still pretty idealistic so this was quite a shock to the system!

The homeless family accommodation primarily consisted of two tenement blocks of flats in Deptford, South London where I was advised to walk under the overhanging passageways because occupants were not averse to throwing unwanted items and refuse over the balconies. Perhaps oddly this experience meant that later, whilst serving in prisons, it came naturally to me to walk under the overhanging walkways, where the danger posed was more likely a chamber pot! This was particularly the case just after Christmas Day, when items ordered from catalogues by our residents (often having used false names and with, of course, no intention of paying), failed to live up to expectation, and were dumped unceremoniously. It was sensible too to always carry a newspaper when visiting, for if invited to sit, one never knew if one was likely to sit on the remains of a meal or the changing of a baby gone awry, for instance.

Frequently the gas and electricity were cut off and coal might be kept in the bath or all doors and frames might be missing – people need heat! These were instances of some families' existence, but of course there were others who were trying to pay off arrears of rent and get re-housed. There was a woman with six children who had just got herself organized, when her husband was released from his latest prison sentence, and to demonstrate his affection tied her to the external passage rails and "caressed" her with his belt! I took a young trainee social-work student to visit, who asked this woman quite out of the blue "Have you tried contraception?" I was shocked at the bluntness; the resident, older, with life experience, just glared.

Another young woman repeatedly got pregnant: each time the resulting child showed signs of personal development, at the age of about twelve months, she lost interest because she simply wanted a doll substitute. Men would often only visit their families at night, sustaining the pretence, so that the woman could continue to receive state benefits. Consequently investigating officers would station themselves to keep watch all night in an effort to frustrate the fraudulent claim. This led on at least one occasion to an angry altercation and me witnessing an assault on an investigator.

I was about to be offered secondment to undertake full time training to become a qualified social-worker, when

I saw an advertisement for training as an Assistant Governor in the Prison Service. I knew that this would involve being posted to prisons around the country, which were likely to be in remote places, and disruption to family life. Initially I was hesitant about applying, but my wife said that she must have some gipsy in her blood for she was happy to have a lifestyle that could involve moving home every few years. Hence I applied, and after a short interview at the old Home Office building in Whitehall (where I duly carried that day's copy of *The Times* (then *The* newspaper)), but not a furled umbrella, I was accepted for training.

3. Initiation

The mood and temper of the public with regard to the treatment of crime and criminals is one of the most unfailing tests of the civilization of any country. Winston S Churchill 1910

I joined the Prison Service at Wakefield Staff College in September 1969 where, after a brief introduction, we were dispersed to placements in prisons. Another trainee and I went to HMP Wandsworth, where we were given a three-week experience of working alongside Prison Officers. As trainee Assistant Governors we were not the most welcome and I remember being told to assist an Officer at unlock (7.30am) on the ground floor ("the ones"). When I approached this elderly grizzled Officer and asked what I should do he said: "I had to find out and you'll have to f...ing do the same". I forget now what I said, but whatever it was he inducted me into the process of handing out and, more importantly, collecting razor blades. Some days later there was a uniformed staff "stick and whistle parade" held between the inner and outer entrance gates, when the Deputy Governor and Chief Officer inspected the rows of staff to check that they had their sticks (i.e. truncheons), whistles and warrant cards. As a trainee in civvies I was at the end of the last row and it happened that the elderly Officer I had "assisted" at unlock stood next to me. Staff held out their sticks etc., except that my neighbour simply held out his clenched fist. As the inspecting management neared, the Officer at the appropriate moment dropped his warrant card and bent to retrieve it. By the time he had picked it up the inspection had moved on! When we were dismissed I complimented him on his timing and got a smile and a lecture on how a rolled up daily paper was far more effective as a weapon. The wooden stick kept in the uniform trouser pocket over time dried out, from body heat, and became so brittle that it was very likely to snap if used. The newspaper jabbed into the solar plexus or face was far more reliable as a weapon on the rare occasion when required, but the useful pocket allowed the paper to be ready for its proper use whenever the opportunity arose. This Officer became quite chatty and told me how he was to retire in a few weeks' time and had no idea where he and his family would live. He had completed twenty-two years in the Army and then joined the Prison Service, all the time living in quarters; there was no way he could afford to buy a house and he was hoping that the local council would provide for him. The sadness of this situation proved to be the beginning of my realization that having accommodation provided by one's employer was, in fact, a mixed blessing, and subsequent experience confirmed this view.

I learned other valuable lessons, which stuck with me – often with a good helping of prison humour! Attached for the morning to the "Centre Office", so called because from it could be seen the length of each wing radiating out from the centre, I was asked by the Centre Principal Officer what was the most important word to be remembered in prison. I admitted to my lack of knowledge on this point whereupon the Officer regaled me with the story of a prisoner who had, a few weeks previously, approached the Centre Office and thrust his head through the glass window, causing severe injury to his head and neck. There was blood everywhere. His deputy, the Senior Officer, calmly looked at the man saying: "There is no need for that lad, there's a door round this side". That is "**imperturbability**"**,** the most important word – whatever happens, do not get flustered.

Another incident brought home to me the unnecessary officiousness exercised by some Officers. Whilst being instructed in the workings of the gate house inner office, I heard the familiar voice of a former colleague announcing himself as "Mr Sanders Probation Officer to see..." I next heard the voice of the Officer on the gate ordering him, in a very unwelcoming and curt manner, to remain on one side of a white line painted on the floor, until told to cross it. I called out "Hello Eddie!" whereupon the attitude of the whole staff changed to one of "Do you know this man?" "Well Sir (to Eddie), do come in". This was another lesson for me in how *not* to treat callers, whether official or not, and emphasizing that the "gate" is the public face of the establishment.

After the prison experience we returned to Wakefield for the academic course. The Mountbatten Report into the escape from Wormwood Scrubs of George Blake had recommended that a significant increase in the number of Assistant Governors should be recruited. There were som fifty trainees on our course, comprising about one third who were direct entrants from university, one third from among serving Prison Officers and the remaining third, like me, who were changing careers. I hated Wakefield and the weekly journey from that city to my home in Faversham, where I had left my wife with two very young children. The course itself was a mixture of sociology, criminology, penal history, prison practice, law and the dreaded essays. One particular remark remained with me, made by a criminology (or perhaps sociology) lecturer, who said we had a choice either to be functionaries of the system or to try to change and improve it – I tried to avoid the former and always attempted to keep in mind the latter, despite institutional pressure.

During this course we were required to do study placements and I did my first in Chesterfield with the Probation Service. Whilst there I joined the office outing to go down Bolsover pit, and that experience, together with a later experience of going down Hatfield coal mine, gave me a great respect for the miners. I also had to supervise cases which entailed home visits and again these were instructive where I found closed mining communities with their own distinctive ethos. We were given some choice with our second (management) placement, and so I agreed with another student to suggest a study of prisoner allocation procedures in the South West Region, arguing that it was a manageable area given the brief period available to us, with a good selection of prisons, which did not have the complications of large urban sprawl. This was accepted. The object of the study was serious, for we suspected that Governors of training prisons would choose at whim from those who were sent by local prisons, who was to stay and who was to get back on the bus. It was all very subjective, inefficient and costly, but governors of these prisons exercised an absolute authority and one of the ways they demonstrated it was by sending so many back to the allocating prison. This caused blockages in the local prisons and destroyed expectations raised with the prisoners concerned. I must confess, we did not declare that choosing the South West also meant that we could rent a house and take our respective families away with us for three weeks at the coast in glorious spring weather!

One experience, which caused me concern, whilst being based at the Verne prison for the duration, was being present at my first Board of Visitors adjudication when a prisoner who had absconded claimed that he had done so due to family matters. After making his plea of mitigation we all left the room whilst the Board considered the punishment to be awarded. Whilst outside the room the prisoner was physically sick, and claimed that whatever he had said the penalty would still be the maximum of 180 days loss of remission – and so it was. The whole procedure seemed a cruel farce.

Towards the end of the course at the posting board I had asked for somewhere near London, because my father had experienced a number of heart attacks and I wished to be within reach. I was posted to Brockhill Remand Centre, situated in the grounds of Hewell Grange Borstal, between Redditch and Bromsgrove in Worcestershire. When I queried this location, given my wish to be near London, I was told that a motorway was in the process of construction! This came back to me years later whilst at Brixton, when the deputy governor recounted his experience of doing detached duty to Northern Ireland, on the understanding that as a Cornishman he could subsequently have a posting in the South West. On his return he was promptly posted to Brixton, London SW2!

4. Apprenticeship 1.

I went to Brockhill Remand Centre as Deputy Governor – and in fact the only other governor grade there other than the No.1. On my preliminary visit the Chief Officer, who had been acting as the deputy, welcomed me, saying that he was pleased to have someone to take the responsibility. The Governor welcomed me by saying: "Sit down Crew. When I say 'jump' every fucker jumps and that includes you." This being my first prison posting I really began to wonder whether I had made the right move. He then took me on a tour of the prison, where we encountered a youth on hands and knees scrubbing the floor. The youth looked up and said: "Good morning sir", whereupon the Governor, who carried a walking stick, tapped the lad lightly across the shoulders saying "Speak when you're spoken to boy". I duly wondered some more! The following day I was received by the Governor who said: "Sit down Crew. There's no way to say this other than to say it straight - your father has died, so you had better cut along home."

A requirement at this time was to live in prison quarters and my rank entitled me to a four bed semi-detached house. The Governor had told me that the house had been let to a Principal Officer on the basis that if a Governor grade was appointed then he would have to move out. Whilst waiting, temporary accommodation would be arranged in Redditch. Subsequently we moved into the official house on the Hewell Grange Borstal estate to find that the Principal Officer (a keen standard rose grower) had taken all his roses with him and left a garden resembling the desolation of a WWI battlefield. One thing about living on such an estate was that labour abounded and the Gardens Party from the Borstal quickly repaired the damage.

Living on this estate was a new experience, for it meant that everyone else was employed either at the

Borstal or the Remand Centre. My wife began taking our young daughter to a playgroup run on the site and when volunteering to join other mothers, fund-raising around the quarters, she recounted her strange experience of calling at a house and being brusquely asked who she was and what she wanted. When she replied that she was the wife of the new Deputy Governor at the Remand Centre, fund-raising for the playgroup, the woman's attitude changed dramatically to become very obsequious (which behaviour my wife found difficult to cope with – as in the armed forces, status by association obviously mattered).

I was very apprehensive at first, however after a few days I had occasion to go into the Governor's office and there he was, perched on a chair on his desk busy rescuing a butterfly which had got caught in the fluorescent light cover. He gently took this to the window and released it – I then began to realize that there was a heart below the hard exterior. Later it became very clear that his hardness was all an act, and I found him a most honourable individual from whom I learned much. Once, when admitting to an error involving a court report, he spoke to the clerk to the court and accepted the blame as if it were his own. When I questioned this he said his view was that as governor, he took responsibility for everything that went on in the prison, and I later learned that his career had suffered a setback when he had accepted full responsibility for the failing of a member of senior staff.

Weekend working, evening and night visits were of course new to me, and it was at Brockhill that I met the occupants who never left a prison despite the attentions of regular visits by the extermination squad. I speak of cockroaches. At the turning on of a light they could be seen scurrying away into the surrounding darkness. They were always particularly numerous around the kitchen and bathhouse, these being hot and moist areas. Later at Brixton I was to see real infestations, where cockroaches existed in this very old building in their thousands. Feral cats and sometimes rats were other institutional problems. The best rat I ever saw was a huge brown glossy example at HMP Oxford – now a hotel!

The Prison Service was at this time split between Officer Grades and Governor Grades and like most newly qualified Assistant Governors, I relied very much on the Principal Officer, who shared my weekends. As a young Officer he had sat with condemned men awaiting execution, was self-taught, loved to quote Shakespeare and had superb management skills exercised with wit and diplomacy. With new arrivals he would line them up, produce a few chicken bones and within minutes spellbind them into emptying their pockets of any items that they had hoped to smuggle in - "kidology" indeed. Another example of this was the Officer who brought on evening / night duty a tape recorder with the sound of a large dog barking, and if lads in their cells got too noisy he would play this and threaten to bring the dog in – this was usually quite effective! Occasionally we would get advance notice from the police – who ferried the youngsters to and from the courts – that a group was rowdy and giving trouble in the van. It transpired that this was all part of the "game" with the police, for once through the gate prisoners knew they had to live with us and there was never any trouble. Most prisoners of course just wanted to get through their time quietly, without bother, for we did not have the serious drugs epidemic of today as a major problem.

Shortly after my arrival the Governor announced that he was taking some holiday and leaving me in charge – still very much with my "L" plates visible. My instructions were to be firm in adjudication and to try to leave him a clear desk on his return. These were the days of dietary punishment so when a lad appeared in front of me for refusing to work I gave "one-day dietary", i.e. bread and water, on the basis that (as I explained) "if you don't work then you don't eat" – they saw the connection. As the Medical Officer said, "A day's fasting is good for the body." I later discovered that the Senior Officer in charge of the Segregation Unit told the youth confined for the day that he was entitled to a book – and promptly handed him an illustrated cookery book. Such is prison black humour. Dietary punishment - more properly called Restricted Diet - of more than three days had to be interspersed with three days ordinary diet, thus nine days (the maximum) Dietary Punishment meant three days bread and water followed by three days ordinary diet, followed by three days bread and water. However one or two days were usually quite sufficient with young lads. Dietary Punishment was ended about a year after I took up post. My view was (and still is) that for young offenders, it is much kinder to give an immediate punishment, which is related to the offence. In the case of delayed punishment (i.e. loss of remission), the punishable offence is often long forgotten by the offender; consequently the added days are bitterly resented.

At the adjudication the youth would be marched in, stood with his back against the far wall opposite me and then the two escorting staff would stand with their backs to me, closely facing the often much shorter prisoner. Obscuring my view of the lad and his of me – the staff took it ill when I asked for sight of the lad – after the hearing they explained that their task was to prevent the lad from assaulting me!

When the governor was away I had the duty of giving a report to the monthly meeting of the Board of Visitors (now the Monitoring Board). They are volunteers, individuals appointed from the local community by the Home Secretary, to oversee the administration of the prison. There was a shortage of staff quarters and Officers might have to wait up to a year before they were allocated a vacant house. At my first meeting with the Board of Visitors I was asked about the length of waiting time, whereupon an elderly retired navy admiral raised himself from his slumber to say "Well, can't you commandeer some then?" I think it was another member who replied to the effect that we were not on a war footing ...

Every few months I noticed that we would have a charge made that an Officer had been assaulted. At that time it was a rare occurrence to have assaults on staff from young lads who were on remand, most wanting any report to court from the prison to be favourable to them. My sense was that one could feel tension arising periodically and that this was only relieved by the "assault", after which tension decreased and staff could again feel that they were doing a dangerous job and were not "soft, caring youth workers" – which in fact they were most of the time.

One event of which I was merely an observer was the incident of the explosives in the lake. 1972 was extremely hot, and the level of the Hewell Grange Lake lowered significantly. The first indication of trouble was when the teachers at the village primary school complained of children taking seemingly live bullets into school. It appeared that at the end of WWII the army unit occupying the Grange simply dumped all spare ammunition that did not feature on the inventory into the lake. The Bomb Disposal Unit arrived, dredged part of the lake, and on finding boxes of assorted ammunition, sought permission of the acting governor of the Borstal as to where to safely explode the stuff. He, so it was reported, simply said "Near the lake". Whether he checked with the Works staff, I know not, but the Army people went ahead and sometime later the good folks of Redditch complained of rising water levels. A hole had been blown in a pipe draining the lake, which then had to be repaired. On a cold dark and windy evening it was the valiant Trades Officers who were trying desperately to create a cofferdam around the underwater hole, from the precarious situation of the institution's canoes.

In 1973 I was transferred to Aylesbury Prison, which held young men whose criminal history was so bad that they had been sentenced to lengthy prison terms. Mostly Borstal "graduates" they were an unpredictable and difficult population. My family followed, moving into the allocated quarter at Bierton a mile or so from the prison and it was at Aylesbury that Martyn was born.

There were, however, as is so often the case in all institutions, moments of great sadness, others of humanity, thankfully few of barbarity and many of sheer hilarity …

- ❖ Visiting a new "reception" of unknown history in his cell, I did what others had joked about yet many had done, and that was to carelessly fail to "spring" the door lock. Thus the door swung shut on us and I became locked in – of course there is no handle on the inside of a cell door - "imperturbability" to the fore I had to ring the cell bell for an Officer to smilingly open up.

- ❖ Sitting uncomfortably on the floor of a cell among shards of glass, with a young man who had just smashed it up, trying to get him to see for himself the pointlessness of bucking the system whilst doing my inadequate best to walk the fine line between empathy (for his wish to express his feelings) and frankly not saying to him that I would have wanted to do exactly as he had done given the injustice from a particular member of staff.

- ❖ Witnessing a Principal Officer sifting through the slops dustbin after a meal, to find a lad's false tooth. This most difficult anti-authority youth, who had a history of violence, looked on in awe that a uniformed Officer would plunge his arm into such a mess – it was beyond his comprehension. His attitude to staff changed and again, it showed that a small event can alter the "them and us" norm.

- ❖ Each Assistant Governor took it in turn to check the discharge dates of prisoners to ensure that they went out on the date according to the court order. On one occasion I found that we had detained a young man some fourteen days beyond his due date. Having got a colleague to double check I took the file to the Governor. Calmly he asked me to bring the individual to him whereupon he told the lad that having made exceptional progress he was to be released forthwith. A delighted young man shortly after walked through the gates to freedom.

- ❖ The prisoner who had marked crosses on each wall of his cell and when asked: "Why not on the ceiling or floor?" said that demons could only exist in a horizontal plane, not in the vertical and hence he did not need protection from above or below. This lad needed to be in a psychiatric hospital, not a prison.

- ❖ The psychiatric report by the elderly ex-military psychiatrist, stating that "this youth has the evil eye". When I queried with him whether this was a medical diagnosis I was told "well he has, hasn't he?"

- ❖ The lad on hunger strike over some issue and the Doctor ordering "No water only milk". When I queried why this should be, I was told that milk furred the tongue and this would cause the lad much discomfort. It is to my shame that I failed to pursue this beyond my immediate superior.

- ❖ Again being called to the prison late one night where a lad had made a self- harm gesture. Blood everywhere, and the Doctor stitching the lad's wrist without (as far as I could tell) any anesthetic, commenting that in his practice outside in the community he had people who "really needed him".

- ❖ The arrival of the first newspaper directed at prisoners indicated it should be shared "one between two". I came onto the wing to find the jovial Senior Officer, respected and seen as a father figure to many, was, with a straight face, tearing each paper across the middle and handing one half to each young prisoner. The lads were taking it all with hilarity.

- ❖ A subsequent Governor who wrote pages for posterity in the daily *Governor's Journal* and who always returned from his daily circuit of the prison via the bathhouse, which caused comment among the inmates. On one occasion my Wing Senior Officer was taking a bath himself having dealt with a dirty protest, when the Governor passed through. He, obviously naked, immediately stood to attention in the bath, clapped his cap on and saluted, stating the usual assertion to a Governor: "All present and correct Sir".

- ❖ This Governor also had the practice of bringing his old Alsatian dog into the Visits Room, about which it would roam wherever its curiosity led. Female visitors were not amused. On one occasion he brought his young son into the prison whilst inmates were seated in the area between the cells watching a film. He left his son just behind the prisoners and went to speak to an officer. The lad, after a while missing his father, turned, expecting to see him by his side. I was concerned at the look of utter panic on his face when he found that Dad could not be seen, and I thought the Governor grossly inconsiderate. He could, though, breed any colour of Budgerigar to order.

Then there was the carpeting of my office: When I arrived at Aylesbury I inherited an office which I considered pretty awful, my main gripe being the linoleum, which was shrunken and cracked, having far outlived its lifespan. I requested a carpet from the Administration Officer who point blank refused to examine the state of the linoleum or even consider the matter. I was furious, and found out from other Assistant Governors that such was this man's attitude to Assistant Governors – albeit he was quite obsequious to the No.1 Governor. My wing staff picked up on this and told me not to worry for there were "ways". Shortly after, following my long weekend off, I returned to find my office carpeted with a lovely royal blue carpet. My Senior Officer winked and said I should not ask questions; just accept that there are "ways". Later in the year the Prison Chapel came to be re-decorated and so it was that when the workmen removed the Altar they found a large square of carpet missing from underneath. They replaced the Altar in its previous position, no questions asked, so all was well. The Chapel carpet was, of course, royal blue.

Months later a shortage of underpants became a cause for concern, staff complaining that they had run out of supplies and that the lads were unable to have a clean weekly issue. Indeed, two to three weeks had already passed with the storemen unable to supply. Naturally, we received no satisfaction from the Administration Officer who was responsible for such provision. However we did learn, upon tackling the store man that underpants were in the stores, but that he was not allowed to issue them because they were of an outdated pattern. My neighbouring Wing Assistant Governor and I decided that we would raid the stores on our next Saturday on duty. This we did, explaining to the duty store man that we were coming in and that he could protest to his boss, the Administration Officer, on Monday morning. Imagine our amazement when we found boxes of underpants (which we duly issued) and an Aladdin's cave of bolts of dress material from the time years previously when the prison had held women prisoners - and among many other items, a veritable pile of carpets just rotting away!

I was the junior Assistant Governor at Aylesbury and whilst the other two of my rank were helpful, and we enjoyed a good relationship, the Deputy Governor was a constant irritant, always finding fault and quite undermining. Being our next door neighbour he would note at what time I left home to do my evening visit and what time I returned, all rather petty. Having already been a Deputy Governor, albeit in a small establishment, I was not about to accept this without standing up for myself, and thus relationships deteriorated. I had responsibility for A Wing and the Induction Unit, but found that the Deputy and the Chief Officer, who often created chaos by agreeing with whatever the last person who saw him wanted, were always interfering and changing things without so much as a "by your leave". My wing team was as angry as I and as a result we became quite a close unit. After I had completed almost two years I had had enough, and asked for a transfer.

I was posted to Brixton within a very short time, so I had already left Aylesbury when I was asked to return for my farewell party. On the morning of the appointed day I received a call at Brixton to tell me that Tom Lemon, my wing Principal Officer, had died unexpectedly, but that the staff had decided that he would have wanted us to go ahead. The party was a farewell to me and a wake for him – I can't remember much about it except that I think most of us slept where we fell and had almighty hangovers the next day. His funeral was the second prison staff funeral I attended at Aylesbury when the procedure was to line the road until the coffin was loaded into the hearse, after which we, the staff, piled into cars and hared along country lanes to beat the arrival of the hearse and again line the roadway and into the chapel. I was, I must confess, very apprehensive at the speed we travelled and very relieved to find that arrangements had been made for the local police to ensure our safe crossing of the various road junctions!

We were allocated a quarter by Streatham Common and settled in. I enjoyed Brixton, for it was the main initial reception prison for all those committed to custody by the London Courts; a complex, extremely busy remand prison of around a thousand prisoners with five hundred staff, who also staffed all the Crown Courts in and around London. A "Can Do Prison", for there was great pride in being able to rise to any reasonable demand. I was again the junior in both rank and service of the five governor grades.

On my arrival at the gate I was welcomed by a Principal Officer whose first words were: "I hope you don't have strange ideas like your predecessor, who wanted things like background music in Reception". I was also informed later of a former No.1 Governor whose wing inspections were considered overly detailed, taking up much of the morning and interfering with the routine. The wing Principal Officer's response was to ensure that there was always some small aspect upon which the Governor would seize, and having done so, would happily speed on his way. On one occasion, allegedly, the Governor on his inspection looked into the bowl of a WC to find a brown blemish, whereupon the Principal Officer put his finger to the mark, put finger to mouth and to the amazement of the Governor and delight of staff said "Sir, It looks like it and tastes like it". "It" was of course peanut butter! This was typical of the humour, which demonstrated the generally high morale I was to find.

My responsibility was the remand wing, comprising some 300 prisoners (mostly three to a cell) and the convicted working party of about 100. The former had to be produced at court weekly, or three weekly, as required. The transport organization and court staffing arrangements, for which I was not responsible, were almost incomprehensible to me but worked like a well-oiled machine. My daily duty was sitting in tandem with the wing Principal Officer interviewing the previous night's "new" receptions ("returners" were seen by the wing Senior Officer); these un-convicted men could number 30 or 40 so the process took most of the morning. I saw there the whole range of human misery and bravura. The rough kindness of staff managing these prisoners, accommodated in grossly overcrowded conditions – there was no in-cell sanitation, just a chamber pot for each man – was amazing.

On one occasion an elderly man came into the room and cowered in the corner, whereupon the Principal Officer went to him, put his arm around him and coaxed his story which was that the man had lost his wife to cancer after many years of marriage and committed his first offence – essentially a cry for help. On another the Principal Officer spent an hour during one reception interview resolving, via RSPCA and other agencies, one man's worries about his budgerigar left in his flat because his solicitor had assured him he would not go into custody – meantime I was continuing to interview the remaining queue! As we received foreign nationals who often spoke no English, it was hilarious to see our extrovert Senior Officer utilizing arm-waving sign language mixed with a few foreign words known to him but expressed in London cockney. Another time dignitaries from the USA visited the cells and were asked who they were by our prisoners. When told, the prisoners immediately began claiming that British prisons were better than American – and this from men three to a cell, each with a chamber pot! You just had to laugh.

Early during my time at Brixton I was attending "Reception", where prisoners are formally handed over to the prison for safe keeping, whilst prisoners were being brought in. Every so often a hand-bell would sound, when I enquired I was laughingly told that when a man had stripped off for the search, if he was particularly well endowed, the bell would be rung. Today this would be regarded as unacceptable, especially following the introduction of women Officers, but at the time this ritual was done as part of the whole relaxed but efficient system which was geared to put men through a bureaucratic process with much rough masculine humour and minimum tension as quickly as possible. It was also the one occasion when I saw a full bottle of whisky poured down the sink – of course it looked like whisky and smelt like whisky but could have been anything!

When we became too overcrowded, I had to select prisoners for drafts to Pentonville prison. Sometimes this would be once or twice a week. This was unpleasant, particularly for south Londoners for it meant great difficulties for their families to visit. Unfortunately it was the expectation of many male prisoners to have, selfishly, their partners visit every day, bringing them tobacco and food - which in those days they could. Visits for the unconvicted were 15 minutes, but this was extended depending upon the queue; however some took advantage and would think nothing of expecting exposure of breasts, or passing of items when kissing. Convicted visits could become even more steamy if allowed by staff inattention, since they were allowed longer but less frequent visits. When we conducted a survey of women who visited to ask them about improving the visiting experience, one thing they were emphatic about was that they did not want more physical privacy with their men folk because they said pressure upon them to co-operate in sexual activity was bad enough and they did not want to visit just for "That".

The convicted men worked in the Officer's mess and in a variety of locations, e.g. the Library, Education, Chapel etc. They were located on the top floor of F Wing, otherwise unkindly known as "Fraggle Rock", because the lower floors were occupied by those hospital patients who were "disturbed". These were very sad individuals being drug addicts, alcoholics, chronic psychiatric cases etc. On one occasion one of these prisoners was choking on his own vomit when a hospital Officer cleared his airway and gave him mouth-to-mouth resuscitation. This was before mouth shields and was one of many instances of staff humanity.

The untimely death of Barry Wiggington (the Governor), was a shock, for he had collapsed after taking a flight in a Tiger Moth plane with a colleague. He was greatly loved and respected and I liked him because I found he spoke, in stockinged feet, to his window plants whilst watering them and had a great sense of humour. On occasion he would pull my leg with "anonymous" notes but I did get a reprimand for stating that it was easier to get a dose of Largactil than a glass of milk – although true in my book, I was allowed to think it but not say it! We knew that he had been a Group Captain during WWII but if asked he would merely say that he had been a driver; if one pressed the point then he admitted that the "vehicle" was a Lancaster Bomber. The issue over the milk was because we were having a number of vegetarians wanting diets suitable for their beliefs. As they explained to me they were happy with "nuts and some milk" but how resentful and obstructive was the Chief Officer Caterer for whom a standard meal, and only a standard meal, was what all prisoners should have. On the other hand if a doctor prescribed a special meal the kitchen would reluctantly have to comply, or for medical reasons a disturbed patient in the hospital would be given a dose of Largactil by the medical staff.

Towards the end of my time I "acted up" as the Courts Governor. This was a liaison role to ensure that our commitments to the Crown Courts were complied with. I was responsible for representing the prison at all the Crown

Courts we served – from Southend to Kingston-on-Thames, and Guildford to St Albans. Together with a Chief Officer we were located in a flat outside the prison on Jebb Avenue, and from there we would independently or together visit the cells area of each court on a random basis, and deal with any problems raised by the Court Administrators. On my first visit to the Central Criminal Court – The Old Bailey – I was taken into the courtroom by the duty Principal Officer to sit in the seat allocated for the Prison Governor. Afterwards, I received a message to attend the presiding Judge Michael Argyle in his room, where I was introduced, welcomed and promptly told that he would comply with any directive given by the prison staff. He had great regard for them in the management of the defendants and the cells area, and if I needed any help from him I only had to ask. Downstairs in the cells area it was as large as a small prison and because it housed many prisoners during the day, it was necessary to provide meals. The prisoners' food was brought from Brixton but the staff, who changed every 20 weeks, appointed their own cook who got his meat from Smithfield and daily provided an excellent menu; so much so that barristers would often prefer to have their meals in the cells area.

At the Court of Criminal Appeal in the Strand there was a Principal Officer and two Officers, the former because of the status of the court and the latter to staff the entry to the cells; staff escorting prisoners from other prisons remained responsible for the appellant. On one occasion the Chief Officer and I visited on a Wednesday, and when we asked the staff how many prisoners were in, they somewhat sheepishly said "none", and then admitted that the court never sat on a Wednesday. This practice had been going on for years without anyone knowing, staff passing the time playing cards or taking turns to go shopping. The practice ended.

On another occasion my colleague responsible for security was summoned with me to attend a judge at St Albans Crown Court. My colleague, having been helped with information by a prisoner, had written to the judge asking for this to be taken into account in sentencing. The judge took exception to this and in his chambers gave us a lecture on the propriety of such a request, and a dressing down. We, having suitably apologized, were then graciously invited to dine with him and his fellow judges.

Our flat was shared with the prison psychologists and once a month on a Friday we cooked ourselves lunch. Having had a previous menu setting session, each of us took on one element of the meal. The No. 9 club (the number of the flat) was always a hilarious occasion because none of us were cooks and it was more by good fortune that we ever sat down to the meal as planned. This, of course, was all done covertly since we started at about 11am and rarely finished before 3pm, when it was time to think about going home, so the "naughty boy" element added to the delight. Later during a full inspection of the prison I could not see how I could explain succinctly the highly complex operation of the court's transport system, whereupon one of the psychologists drew a diagram somewhat similar to the London Underground map, which connected all the courts, staffing and transport routes – just brilliant.

When I came to leave Brixton I was approached in my office by a store man who, to my surprise, presented me with a box of stationery items, saying that he was aware that I was going to a remote country Borstal and such items could be useful. This was at a time when one had to return an empty biro in order to be issued with a new one, when it was almost impossible to get sellotape and when a fluorescent tube had been taken out of each light fitting to make necessary economies. It transpired that this kindness was a result of me having lent a hand at some time to two struggling store men trying to get a filing cabinet up some awkward stairs – strange how a small helpful gesture can be remembered and repaid!

Lowdham Grange – Arrival of the marchers from Feltham Borstal 1980

Lowdham Grange senior staff on the retirement of Governor Frank Mitchell. Me centre i/c bottle

5. Apprenticeship 2

I was promoted in 1978 and posted to Lowdham Grange as Deputy Governor. This was the first "open" Borstal founded in 1930 after a march from Feltham, of which more later. We took up residence at 1 The Green on the Borstal estate, a large five bedroomed detached house where we were to spend the next five years.

My predecessor had, it transpired, created divisions between governor grades and staff and had not related well to the Governor, a kindly man coming up to retirement. After I had demonstrated that, as the Regional Director said "it was the Governor's job to state the ship's destination and the Deputy Governor's job to get her there", I was fully in accord with this philosophy and having got the junior governor grades (housemasters) on board, we developed a relatively harmonious management team. Unfortunately, as I later found, where management was or had been insensitive, lacking or divided there was always a union activist who stepped in to provide leadership, with self-interest as a prime objective. It was then a challenge to wrest back management control. Having arrived from Brixton where the whole issue was most professionally managed, I found this disquieting. When the Prison Officers Association (POA) had a meeting with the Governor it was held in the Governor's office, which was also the boardroom. When the Board of Visitors met, the tables were re-arranged so that everyone sat formally around the enlarged table, however when the Governor met with the POA, chairs were lined up facing the Governor's desk. This, whilst easier, had the appearance of the union reps being supplicants in the headmaster's study. Given that the POA secretary had a tendency towards confrontation this format was not conducive to ease relationships and, perhaps, was one of the causes which led eventually to significant periods of industrial action over a staffing related issue.

More cheerfully, Lowdham had able staff committed to the development and training of the young offenders. Staff at the time wore civilian clothes but later, because the prison service refused to increase the clothing allowance in line with inflation, uniforms were issued. The main difference was that good officers remained good officers but poor officers relied on the authority of their uniform; also, whereas before everyone of whatever rank had tended to muck in, the "pips" on the shoulder emphasized rank and job demarcation became much more noticeable.

As elsewhere, there were the humorous events to remember:

- It was fairly common for the caterer when baking doughnuts to send a sample to me for afternoon tea. On one particular afternoon a Trainee arrived at my office with a cake; it was a cream cup cake (something I was not partial to), so I suggested that Nick Plumbridge, a newly arrived Assistant Governor who was with me, might like it. He accepted and duly ate it. The lad's face was a picture. After the lad had gone I asked Nick why the lad had looked quite startled. Nick said the cake had been filled with shaving foam but there was no way he was about to let on in front of the boy. As a result Nick's reputation was greatly enhanced.

- Every April 1st a lad would be sent to the stores for a packet of water powder, and every year one fell for it and actually went to ask the storeman.

- Again April 1st. An Assistant Governor, kept a number of caged birds in a disused bedroom. His Principal Officer conned him into believing that the birds had laid eggs – the eggs were very realistic but when one was "accidentally" dropped – of course they were made of wood. On another occasion, he ran to attend an alarm bell thinking an incident had occurred; when he arrived at the scene a trainee told him he had been "had". My colleague, who was not about to let this pass, promptly informed the boy that he was being charged with wasting time and escorted him to the Segregation Unit. At the gate of the unit he turned to the quaking youth and told him that he had been "had" in return!

- Trainees were paid in cash but could not have more than 50p at one time in their possession, with which they could purchase small items from the Canteen. One enterprising Gardens Officer, when a difficult piece of ground had to be cleared, would strew a handful of pennies across the area as an incentive – and it certainly worked.

- Whilst attending a meeting of the Board of Visitors and giving my report, the door to the boardroom opened a few inches and a hand holding a milk bottle with a large red rose appeared at floor level. It placed the bottle on the floor and the door silently closed. "The great and the good" looked at me in puzzlement. The penny dropped and I had to admit to it being my birthday.

- The lad who had smashed up the Segregation Unit cell. Whereas my previous experience had been to let the occupant tire himself before entering, I was surprised when a Principal Officer entered and proceeded to give the lad a hug. Tears and all well - if you know whom you are dealing with.

- The trainee who kept absconding: the Governor said that he was not inclined to transfer the lad to a closed Borstal for he felt there was "something to the youth". His Assistant Governor suggested to me that when I next adjudicated on him I should tell him that I was not going to extend his stay but start giving him time back. It worked - the lad never absconded again – he was actually scared of being discharged. Another lesson in the impact of institutionalization and the fear of facing the difficulties of resettlement.

- In fair weather lads were allowed to take their visitors onto the Sports Field to watch a game if in progress or more often to walk and talk. It was said that many a young man learned to escape the eye of staff and wander with his girl into the adjacent woods, where other activities were pursued!

- The trainee who absconded in the snow and left a nice trail of footprints to follow!

- Another lad absconded several times. I took the attending officers with the young man outside the Segregation Unit, and said that I was fed up with him putting everyone to trouble at night, and would give him five minutes to run if that was what he really wanted. The staff plainly thought I was mad. We all stood in silence, one could feel the tension building in the youth and once or twice I thought my gamble might not pay off. However after about three minutes of silence he broke down and wept. He stayed the course.

- One summer night a night patrol reported a trainee missing from a dormitory. The absconder procedure was activated. Sometime later another lad in the dormitory said that he had heard noises from outside the window. Sure enough there was our missing young man asleep on the window verandah. He claimed that he had been too hot inside so climbed out for fresh air and had gone to sleep.

- Many lads had never seen cows and were often found talking to the young calves. Trainees involvement with the cows and pig-rearing unit often helped to break through the carapace of hardness which some had when they came to Lowdham.

- There was one tragedy when a lad vaulting over a horse in the gym fell and broke his back. At the hospital the Consultant said that it was a pity that he had not died, for he would be paralysed from the neck down. As far as I know, the then Governor was still in touch with the lad some twenty years later.

- There was also an incident when a trainee had his back severely lacerated requiring some 48 butterfly stitches. The subsequent enquiry showed that he had persuaded another youth to tie him to a chair and inflict the wounds with a Stanley knife blade because he was due to attend a court of appeal hearing, and misguidedly thought that to present himself as being the subject of an attack would gain sympathy from the judge. The court, understandably, was not impressed.

In 1980 an Assistant Governor, suggested the re-enactment of the march from Feltham to Lowdham with some staff and Borstal trainees, to mark the 50th anniversary of the establishment. In 1930 a party of staff and lads had marched from Feltham to live under canvas whilst they assisted tradesmen in building the first "open" Borstal where young men would live on trust. Sir Alexander Paterson had said that "You cannot train people for freedom whilst keeping them in captivity", and Lowdham was the experiment. At a staff meeting our Chaplain, breezily announced to gales of laughter, that he would have a huge erection outside the Gym to welcome the walkers back on their arrival! Of course he actually meant a huge cross, and a dais with the Bishop et al. We enlisted the assistance of the TocH organization (whose own origins make a story in itself), which had arranged the accommodation for the marchers in 1930, and they magnificently arranged the accommodation en-route again. To the credit of all concerned the march was a huge success raising some £2000 in aid of Jimmy Savile's fundraising for Stoke Mandeville Hospital. Subsequently myself, the instigator of the re-enactment and two members of staff together with a few trainees went to be present at Savile's programme, at the BBC. Most of the lads who had never been to London were quite overwhelmed by seeing some of the sights, especially Downing Street. I doubt it could be done nowadays with the politicization of prisoner treatment – or with the subsequent exposure of Jimmy Savile.

A regular springtime treat was to "beat the bounds". The Chief Officer, Farm Manager and I would walk a circuit of the estate limits – a distance of some four or five miles, breaking for lunch at the village pub in Epperstone before the last mile back to the main Borstal buildings. Christmas too was quite a different event. Although it was customary in most prisons that the Governor did Christmas Day and the Deputy did Boxing Day, it was hinted that it would be taken amiss if I did not put in an appearance myself. Since we all lived on site, the Governor and his wife would tour the houses during Christmas morning wishing everyone a Happy Christmas and partaking of a glass with the house staff. Alcohol was not allowed for trainees but staff would have a bottle or more of some refreshment in the house office and I was given, as it turned out, good advice to start at the house farthest from my quarter. Some staff brought their wives in and at lunch time staff served the trainees at their tables. This tradition (borrowed from the Armed Forces where officers serve their men) was a useful insight which I was later to value at Askham Grange.

Each house had its own take on "a Christmas drink". I started at Paterson house where I was invited into the office for a sherry – all very proper and sedate. Next in Malone house I was offered a large sherry, which was topped up. Then feeling warmed up and beginning to think of my Christmas dinner to come, it was on to Warner house. There it was deemed that sherry was a ladies' drink so it was whisky – a large one. And then finally to Stansfield house where the choice was comprehensive. Having just had whisky I elected for another – it came in a small tumbler three quarters full. Whilst conversing I put the glass still a quarter full on a table. When I went to pick it up there was a fresh glass refilled. As I left I noted that the trainees on the house seemed very eager to wash up the "empties" – they all seemed to be in a very merry mood too!

I was duly posted in 1984 (I had probably stayed at Lowdham too long but it was an excellent place for my children to grow up) to become Deputy Governor at Gloucester, a local county gaol. The Governor had just sold off the only suitable quarters so for the first time since Faversham we had to buy a house which, as it turned out was helpful because it forced us to get on the housing ladder to ownership.

Gloucester Prison was like going back in time. Collusion between staff and prisoners – who had known each other over the generations, it seemed, and also the police. I had not been there long when returning from lunch I was preceded by a man who rang the gate bell, and when the Officer opened it the man said "The copper's just following. I have been remanded". The policeman duly arrived after a few minutes! Conducting my first reception board, I arrived in the interview room to find just one chair behind the desk. When I asked for another chair I was asked why I needed one. Upon replying "For the prisoner", I was met with utter amazement that I should allow a prisoner to sit for interview, a custom we had always practiced at Brixton (a much busier prison), and anyway more civilized and conducive to dialogue.

Although substituting for the Governor I was also responsible for the Rule 43 wing. This was a segregated unit holding some eighty primarily sex offenders. As a father myself it was with some misgiving that I approached this task. The great majority were very inadequate, immature human beings, many of whom could not relate to women, with a few who were truly of "evil" intent. I had to write reports on these men at intervals relating to their fitness for an "open" prison or for parole. One individual calmly told me how he had sexually abused his daughter for years since she was quite young and this had been his regular practice since ... but he told me that he always left some payment on the mantelpiece – some justification! He was not alone for many excused their behaviour similarly – and it was a revelation to me how many mothers refused to face the issue and turned a blind eye, disbelieving that their men-folk could do such acts and sometimes blaming their daughters who in turn suffered guilt at breaking up the family. Quite a dynamic to digest!

As in other prisons there was much humour, and also sadness. One young man had been a disturbed patient on the hospital wing but had formed a calming relationship with a hospital Officer. Shortly after his release this young man took a gun into the local police station and took a hostage, our hospital Officer offered to negotiate but was refused by the police. Subsequently the young man shot himself.

As a local prison we were required from time to time to take prisoners from training prisons for a "lie down". Essentially this meant taking a particularly troublesome prisoner for a few weeks to give the staff at the training prison a rest and to remind the prisoner that the conditions he enjoyed in his home establishment were to be valued. Of course, once received it became difficult to transfer them back because there was always a reason why the home establishment should find cause for delay. However one man serving a life sentence for the murder of a policeman, both of whom had been 19 years old at the time, kept himself to himself when he first came. Sometime later he saw another prisoner attacking a member of staff and intervened to save the Officer: when asked why he had done so, he simply said that staff had been fair to him during his stay. He suffered no repercussions from the prisoners because of his Lifer status and he asked if he could stay with us.

During my time at Gloucester I became involved in assisting to set up the local Victim Support Scheme and as a volunteer I took my turn visiting victims of crime. On one occasion I went to a house in a poor part of the city where I found a careworn young woman with very young children: they had been burgled, and among other things taken was the TV. She said that her husband had gone "up town to get a loan", not for food it transpired but to replace the TV! As I left her husband returned and we realized we knew each other – I had seen him discharged from the prison days earlier.

After I had been about a year in post a new Governor arrived and shortly after he was required to instigate budget savings. The POA chairman said that he was not concerned with management's problems and would not see a penny taken from the Officers' pockets. Industrial action inevitably followed. In the early stages, staff simply told prisoners to sit down on the exercise yard and refuse to come in at the appointed time. This manipulation of prisoners was blatant and quite disgraceful, however such was the nature of the historical collusion – Governors came and went but Officers were there for the long haul! The next incremental step was the staff disobeying the daily routine orders for the running of the prison, the Governor and myself simply disregarded - effectively mutiny, a term subsequently supported by the Chief Inspector of Prisons in his enquiry but reduced to Disobedience of Orders during an Industrial Dispute by HQ. Shortly before a number of Gurkhas were said (controversially) to have mutinied. They had been dismissed, so presumably to have maintained the mutiny charge without sacking the officers was not deemed to be in the public / political interest.

    The Governor made arrangements for other governor grades to be assembled outside the prison, and I was required to go out during the evening on the pretext of getting fish and chips for our refreshment but in reality to brief the assemblage. The result was that I knocked at the gate; when it was opened we all quickly entered and the Governor told the Officers that he was taking over the running of the prison. The next day, staff were told that they could return to duty if they signed to accept the authority of the Governor but on the instruction of their Union declined to do so.. The Governor decided that prisoners were better out of their cells, which although rowdy brought most of them to see our good faith. I remember breaking into the gym store to provide some footballs for a kick around in the yard – they went over the wall quite quickly. The kitchen party with a young female governor in charge provided meals, and the men mostly crowded around the television sets watching the news of several other prisons having their disturbances – most comments were to the effect "I am glad we're not there". The Chaplain sat outside the prison gate to deal with the anxieties of relatives and friends. A few prisoners did take advantage to cause disruption, primarily by breaking through onto the roof and proceeding to throw missiles down onto anyone who moved below – hard hats were the norm when outside. During one cold night a couple of prisoners came down from the roof and said to the duty Governor that they were all willing to come down on certain conditions – the short reply was to the effect that there were no conditions to be negotiated, they could stay out in the cold. Some suggestions were made that a dowsing with a fire hose might add encouragement, but were rejected on safety grounds. Several days then followed with governors running the gaol whilst striking Officers climbed scaffolding outside the wall to shout to prisoners, telling them not to obey us.

Having worked with these men for some two years I was distressed at the turn of these events and in the absence of any apparent end to the dispute, with the assistance of my wife, I formulated the first draft of a document which tried to bring resolution whilst enabling each side to retain some "face". After a number of meetings involving POA NEC members, the local committee and the Governor, and a number of re-drafts of my paper, an agreement was signed. On the way home I felt tears running down my face and I had to pull over to regain my composure; I had never felt the after effects of stress before. The end of my invincible macho days! After the industrial action feelings were still high and negative towards me because I was seen to have supported the Governor and had been instrumental in taking over the Gate. It was therefore agreed that my departure would be appropriate.

During much of 1988 I undertook detached duties at a number of prisons. Firstly Long Lartin where I gained a limited experience of the tensions in running a maximum security prison and witnessed the crudity and divisiveness of the governor (from whom I had taken over as Deputy at Lowdham Grange). I also worked at South West Regional Office, Bristol Prison and Rolleston Camp, the latter an army camp being used as a temporary prison.

During this nomadic period I was placed on the list for promotion to Governor 3. After an interview whereby I briefly met His Hon. Judge Tumim, Chief Inspector of

Prisons, and was then passed around the team members who unbeknown to me notified the Judge that they approved, on my return to his office he agreed to my becoming his Staff Officer.

Judge Tumim rightly attained public acclaim for his critique of the prisons the teams inspected. Generally he opened the inspection by touring the prison with the Governor (upon whom he would pass a snap opinion), and then later meeting separately a group of staff and a group of prisoners. The inspecting team would spend three or four days interviewing and examining all aspects of the prison. At the closure of the inspection he would listen to all the evidence presented by each member of the team, test it in open forum and then write the verdict. Whilst his strength was that as a legal mind he stressed that the recommendations to be made must fall out of the evidence and though he could be kind, his man management was nil. He treated his driver, secretaries and anyone who would not stand up to him quite without patience or consideration at times having no realization that he was doing so. He subsequently, allegedly, found me difficult because I was, in his opinion, too old for the post I occupied and he really wanted young acolytes around him who would not question his pronouncements. Also I think he was aware that I lacked patience with his politicking and temperamental self-promotion; I had noted this egotism before when politicians had visited prisons. As a result I spent more and more time assisting the inspecting teams, which I enjoyed, and where I picked up much that was to be useful to me later on.

Askham Grange Prison. The first open prison for women, opened 1947.

6. Governing

In 1991 I was asked to spend a couple of weeks standing in for the Governor of Askham Grange, who had been off sick for some time. I remember sitting in a lay-by within sight of the prison, composing myself and thinking of *Twelve O'Clock High,* an old Gregory Peck film (where I had seen him do this himself prior to taking command of an air squadron). I reflected that under my belt I had experience in administration, youth work, homeless families, work in almost every type of male prison, considerable experience of industrial relations and disputes and frequently acting up for the governing governor as well as inspecting. I had also undertaken courses in management, finance, project management, hostage management etc.etc. I felt reasonably confident that two or three weeks in charge of a prison for women should be a walkover. How wrong I was, what a learning curve and what, eventually, became the most rewarding period of my career.

On entering the prison I was met by the departing temporary governor who wished me well, saying that he was glad to be leaving such a madhouse and returning to the sanity of a male prison – the fact that it was a maximum security prison posed my first niggle of unease. Askham, an open prison for women was, in its physical environment a delight – see *"The Story of a House"*[1] - but it was, in management terms, drifting and without direction in the absence of the Governor who had been covered by a succession of temporary reliefs. As I had previously experienced when management abdicated or was absent, the POA filled the vacuum and usually there was an activist with an axe to grind; Askham was no exception.

The prison had a number of staff who had been in post for years, and had never served elsewhere. Again it was like going into a time warp. Women prisoners scrubbed floors on their knees whilst Officers stood over them (hospitals and other institutions had given up the practice in favour of long-handled swabs or electric polishers, years before), the administrative staff worked at tiny desks which may have been official issue when clerks wrote memos in long hand, but were totally inadequate for computers, and the kitchen served boiled rice for pudding every other day without any variation or flavouring etc. What shocked me in particular was that only staff were permitted to use the main staircase whilst prisoners had to use the "back stairs", i.e. the servants' stairway! The number of women placed on Governors' Report every day was excessive and the Board of Visitors, in my view, exacted punitive amounts of remission upon those who were referred to them. But I had my own personal lavatory!

When I arrived the Deputy Governor lectured me that if I didn't know about the wiles of women I would quickly learn and discover the use to which they put their various orifices for secreting forbidden items. Whilst this instruction was in process, a Senior Officer entered the office and upon being introduced told me that I was not there to idle my time but to do some work! I was beginning to understand what my predecessor had meant. Worse was to come when I discovered the attitude of the POA secretary, who seemed adamant that whatever "management" proposed they had an ulterior motive and as such it was to be resisted, regardless of merit. I later discovered that she was allegedly having an affair with a member of the POA National Executive, and it was in both their interests to have industrial relations problems so that he had cause to visit.

In typical HQ style it became apparent that I was going to be left in charge of the prison until such time as the Governor returned to duty. But events were conspiring against me because I was leaving home in Gloucester every Sunday evening and returning Friday evening, which undoubtedly added to the stress of attempting to manage an establishment for which I had no long-term responsibility and which in my view had lost the spirit of adventure and innovation which had inspired its creation. In consequence I suffered, at the age of 52, a heart attack. Thankfully I recovered and in so doing led those in the "Ivory Tower" to make the decision that between myself and the Governor, it would be worth giving me Askham and posting him to HQ. Fortunately I had not long returned when the POA activist achieved a posting too, which removed one major obstacle.

After confirmation of my taking charge we moved to North Yorkshire which was, I was told, "The Centre of the Universe" or "God's Own Country" – as a Londoner I found that the natives actually believed it! Invited to a Reception in York I was enlightened by one individual who said "We had a Parliament before London". In fact I found it to be quite true that the natives are indeed friendly and do laugh at themselves – when admitting their reputation as "careful" it is said (but not true) that "A Yorkshireman is like a Scot but without the sense of humour". Our children had flown the nest when we moved to North Yorkshire. My mother who had come to live with us in Gloucester came too, but after a time moved into a home, and subsequently died. My involvement in Askham and my wife's developing interests (which I did not share) led to a period of what I termed "marital inertia" and eventually to us going our separate ways.

It was relayed to me that the staff thought that I had been posted in from the Inspectorate to shut the prison, because its prisoner numbers had been declining and it was at the time only half of its full capacity of 130. I held a staff meeting, explained that it was my intention to stay for at least three years if allowed to and that I hoped we could make efforts to make the prison viable. Having asked for ideas I was amazed to find that the Senior Officer who had met me with the exhortation that I was expected to work, herself had the Officers together *during their lunch period* to come up with ideas. As a result we sent out mixed teams of staff and prisoners to local prisons, particularly Holloway and New Hall, to seek out prisoners who might be eligible to come and to sell Askham to them. We began to fill up. The arrival of a significant number of foreign nationals who had been sentenced – mostly for being "mules", i.e. trying to smuggle drugs, added to our numbers, and also to our diet and ethnic awareness – as they said, they were a thousand miles from home so to be two hundred miles from London was no problem.

Staff at Officer level were entirely female, and had often been promoted in-situ, thus compounding the inward looking perspective. Women Officers had been introduced into male prisons some years previously (not without misgivings from male Officers). However, it quickly became apparent that their presence had a civilizing and calming effect (on both staff and prisoners) and that they were wholly competent in physical manhandling when so required. It seemed to me that at a time when equality was being promoted that a few male officers might create a more normal environment. I was aware that there would be problems to be overcome but I was surprised at the vehemence against any rational consideration of the matter. Of course I had come to appreciate that many of the women, both prisoners (and staff) had been abused by men but it seemed more that this was a cultural change for which staff were not ready, so it went on the "back burner" for the time being. However I was determined to bring in fresh blood when senior vacancies occurred and when an officer attained promotion I resisted their wish to stay and encouraged them to try another experience. On a couple of occasions they told me that they would apply to return after a suitable period gaining experience elsewhere – of course they never did, having learned to fly!

The Area Manager in our first meeting said that the place primarily needed leadership, and that he would back me in order to bring Askham forward into the current decade. He was as good as his word and provided some funding from which we were able to replace office desks, dining room furniture and carpeting. The latter caused some debate. Whilst it was recognized that the linoleum was well past its life, carpet was viewed, by some, as an unnecessary luxury. However, when it was explained that carpeting was cheaper and that in a melee it was softer to fall upon, Officers objections disappeared. The monotonous diet was more difficult to deal with and was only eventually resolved when the caterer retired.

There was also the issue of lesbian relationships openly among staff, which was novel to me in that at that period - 1990s - in the macho world of the male prison no Officer would admit to being gay. At Askham, prisoners were definitely NOT allowed to indulge in such practices. One of the early policies I had to argue through was when did "friendly cuddling" become a sexual act? In dormitories where most of the women slept, we eventually settled on "Okay on top of the bed covers but not underneath" – in my view it was simply a matter of decency for the other occupants. After the initial fuss everything calmed down without further problem, and it meant fewer governors' reports. My view became that men internalize feelings but women, especially when missing children or undergoing stress, turn to physical contact more easily, and it is wrong to read too much into this. Indeed as someone pointed out to me that the "wiring and plumbing are different" to my previous life expectations in male prisons!

Infringements of prison rules was another long-term issue and remained so until a new (male) Senior Officer suggested that we should adopt something similar to staff disciplinary procedures i.e. a verbal, then a written warning and then formally placement on Governors' Report – albeit with the proviso that an Officer could go direct to a formal report if the offence warranted. These infringements of rules most frequently involved disobeying an order, and this pointed up yet another difference between the sexes. Men almost invariably took the view that one simply obeyed the last order and even in the midst of a task given by one Officer would naturally obey a subsequent order given by another, whether or not the current task was left unfinished. Women would not mean to disobey, but would argue to defer the change of task until the first had been completed. Having thought about this it seemed to me that women, especially if at home with children, were more used to self-managing their time, e.g. choosing their own daily routine etc. So in fact disobedience was rarely actually intended. This system of warnings turned out to be a great success, being seen as fair by both staff and prisoners.

As for the Board of Visitors I simply stopped referring any but the most serious matters to them, but consulted on a whole range of policies and strategic issues and used them as a sounding board. As a result we respected each other's differing roles and I cannot emphasize how much I owe to them for their independence, critical friendship and continually helping me to develop ideas. I read *Prisons I Have Known* by Mary Size, the governor brought out of retirement to open Askham in 1947; also Joanna Kelley's (the second governor) book *When the Gates Shut* and reminiscences of the early days of East Sutton Park Borstal, all of which helped me to gain a historical perspective and which enforced the idea of a "family" community. As a consequence I felt that my primary task was to "set the tone", encouraging the development of a "family" environment where all staff and prisoners would be treated courteously as individuals, contributions for improvements considered and (if acceptable) developed. However the survival of the institution had to be paramount, for as a small prison we had to demonstrate cost effectiveness, i.e. discharging women who did not re-offend and, of course, staff jobs depended on its success.

The office I inherited was immediately by the main entrance. As such, everyone had access to me, meaning line managers were often ignored and I was plagued for answers to the most insignificant of decisions. My usual answer was "What would you do?" It was obviously a lack of confidence, which was underlined when I passed an Officer conversing with a group of prisoners and she came running after me to apologize for talking with them. Her relief and liberation when I said that this was what I expected her to do was obvious. Thus I moved my office up to the Administration corridor above the ballroom – yes we had a ballroom - and beneath that a swimming pool, the latter to be converted into a gym eventually. After this my old office became a conference room, and kicked off the development of the prison as a host for meetings. My being just that slightly more remote, meant that I, the Administration staff and by now, the prisoners, all used the main staircase and were open to staircase conversations. This meant that staff used line managers more, and it encouraged communication at appropriate levels and confidence in their own judgement among staff at all levels.

Of the departments which make up the small town that is a prison, the Works Department is vital and thankfully this operated well, with Trades Officers going about their work accompanied by one or two prisoners learning some practical skills. The Education Department had just had the acting manager appointed in charge and she was keen to develop opportunities for the women to gain useful practical skills which interested them. This led to dressmaking, where children's clothes and other garments (including underwear, which led to the teacher becoming known as the "Knicker Lady") were fashioned, a catering course which eventually developed much admired conference buffets, a business studies course and a hairdressing salon with a huge benefit to the grooming of prisoners and staff who acted as guinea pigs – only one disaster when somebody had an unasked for vivid green tint! Those of academic bent were often placed at York College or University, and at Askham Bryan Agricultural College.

It was, and presumably still is, a duty of the Governor to daily taste the meals provided to prisoners, and I had always done this by visiting the kitchen where a meal was offered for this purpose. Our kitchen was sorely in need of modernisation and it was decided to relocate the kitchen. When this was done, the lay-out made it much easier simply to queue with the women, take a meal and find a vacant chair at one of the tables with them - always seeking permission. During all the meals that I enjoyed in social conversation there was never any attempt by them to use the situation, having "got the Governor captive", just the surprise and curiosity of new arrivals as to who I was.

The Chaplaincy worked, as an interfaith team, quietly and harmoniously, as did both the Gardens and Administration Departments. However the Probation Team caused me concern for in a population of women, many damaged and stressed, it seemed to me entirely inappropriate that all three Officers, however kindly, were men. Taking this up with the Chief Probation Officer I was told bluntly that "A Probation Officer is a Probation Officer is a Probation Officer." Insensitive in my book, for if a woman has a choice to see a female doctor to discuss intimate issues she similarly has a right to see a female Probation Officer. The Probation Inspectorate immediately understood my point when I approached them, but asked that I have patience for a month or two. The Chief Officer was about to retire, unbeknown to me, and this paved the way to achieve a more balanced team since the new incumbent and I struck up a positive relationship, and at his suggestion we jointly interviewed all future applicants.

Later the appointment of a female Senior Probation Officer created a whole new dynamism in the unit, which became a force with great input into the regime of the prison. We also re-located (as we had done with the Medical Centre), the Probation team to a disused house within the grounds in order to try to normalize the fact that people have to make an effort to visit for a service.

Gradually staff gained confidence in me, and I in them, and in turn they gained confidence in themselves. It took a while and some "stand offs" for the POA representatives to appreciate that I was determined to manage in my own way, but would do so by listening to them and dealing fairly with issues raised. Later I felt able to recommend three members of staff for Honours, of whom two were awarded the MBE – one being the Senior Officer who had first told me that I was expected to work, not idle! Gradually I also became more confident in myself within this environment and began to enjoy the challenge of moving the prison forward – or perhaps back – to what had been envisaged in 1947. I was much heartened by the fact that the majority of staff welcomed the idea of becoming a centre of innovation, flexibility and considered risk taking. When given the basic idea of what I was about, and freedom to exercise their initiative, staff members were happy to use their imagination and humanity to assist women dealing with their often complex problems. I was supported throughout my tenure by several able Deputy Governors without whose efforts I could never have achieved little on my own.

On my first night visit I was surprised to find the external doors locked. When I queried this in an open prison I was firmly told that it was not to keep the women in, but the men out. I was learning! On one occasion a young man thought it funny to drop his trousers and "do a moonie", unfortunately his getaway was not fast enough for he was caught, taken into the prison and told that he would not be reported to the police but was being handed over to the women prisoners. This caused him such fear and panic that he was "allowed" to escape and never was seen again.

When asked by a woman in the Mother and Baby Unit if she might have some sparklers sent in for November the 5th, we naturally discussed the health and safety issues. Someone came up with the idea of a bonfire and set piece fireworks, so that all could enjoy. A Senior Officer volunteered to run a hotdog stand and the Gardens Officer volunteered to do the fire and fireworks. The villagers were also invited. The highlight for me was a prisoner who thanked me, saying that she never expected to enjoy any aspect of prison and had spent one of the best evenings of her life.

As we approached December, the question arose as to my policy regarding home leave over Christmas. It seemed to me that mothers were better home with their children, and better for the children, than fretting inside, so for as long as I was able we sent everyone home we could. I always tried to keep in mind that by depriving children of their mother those children could well be the criminals of tomorrow. This meant for the early years we had fewer than twenty residents for whom we tried to give as good a time as possible. We never had a failure to return, and in fact one heavily pregnant woman (after checking with our doctor) whom we had allowed to travel to London, went into labour on her return rail journey somewhere in the Leicester area but hung on until she arrived back in the prison. We just got her to York Hospital in time for the birth. When asked why she had not got off the train she replied that she did not want to let us down! After the crack-down on Home Leave generally I had to use a little more discretion – it helped being remote from HQ and their lack of interest in the Women's Estate!

I was frequently asked whether I was in favour of reintroducing the Christmas Pantomime, which in the past had brought villagers into the prison. However, the number of short sentence women meant that rehearsals would be a nightmare to organize so the Education Department suggested a Fashion Show. Women made their attire in class and what a production ... the only slight snag was that the "bride" was successful on appeal two days before the show and obviously took her dress with her. The teacher and volunteers made a bridal outfit out of muslin and whatever was to hand and the show went ahead. Staging for the ballroom catwalk was borrowed, villagers came as well as all who wanted. In other years we had both Summer and Winter Fêtes with proceeds going to charity.

Christmas was also the time when we received many cards from former residents. The messages that always got a cheer were from women who wrote to say that they had found the courage to "leave him". This was another steep learning curve, which I had to undergo. At male prisons, women would travel enormous distances at great inconvenience to visit their men folk. I found that men would make promises to visit, women would go to great lengths to be presentable and then they would sit and wait and wait and then some quiet crying – there would then be the excuse that the car had broken down or some other pathetic reason. My first adjudication on a woman who was late returning from a day release in York led, on enquiry, to the discovery that she had had a row with her partner and had followed him to the station pleading with him not to take his anger out on the children. I cannot remember the punishment I handed out but asking the Officer after whether I had been led up the garden path she replied: "Did you see the scars around her neck? I could not help but notice. I was then told that this partner had put petrol soaked rags around her neck and had set them alight. Asking why any woman would stay with such a man the reply was "For some women any man is better than no man". I was shaken to find that not only the economics of leaving a relationship (especially with dependent children) were difficult, but also that the whole dynamics of control and submission were a dimension in which I might have to quickly gain knowledge.

Staff training was needed to widen the experience of other establishments. I included a mix of staff from different departments and together with one or two Board of Visitors' representatives we toured Scottish prisons and later arranged a very welcoming visit to the Republic of Ireland. Also on the list was Newton Aycliffe, to see conditions young people under prison age were held and where I first met the young lady who was to come to us towards the end of her sentence and whose poem "Myself" I add later in the book. Some of us also visited other prisons for women around the country. An early visit to Foston Hall where duvets had been introduced led us down the same path. Other ideas led to the re-introduction of visits outside in the gardens when the weather allowed.

Visiting parties of magistrates were often surprised at the ethos and living conditions, the (mostly) ladies from the Shires occasionally remarking that they paid thousands of pounds to send their children to educational establishments with far more Spartan conditions. It had to be explained that the loss of liberty was **the** punishment required by law. My view being that we aimed to provide a challenging yet basic guest house accommodation where residents would be safe, treated with decency and could be warm, sleep comfortably and have enough to eat ; for who is able to motivate themselves to learn or work if deprived of these basics? It was however true that the cost to the State of keeping someone in prison was greater than any Public School, and if realized by the taxpayer perhaps there would be more regard given to not filling prisons with so many males and females who did not need incarceration.

Eventually when it seemed appropriate we took on two male Officers who by their attitude and respect for the women demonstrated the "good" representatives of their sex. The younger who was a family man himself was a hit on the Mother and Baby Unit, often seen with child in arms. I also tried to encourage Officers to wear civilian dress when inside the prison and some did – others complained that this meant they had to choose something different each day, proving I think that women dress for each other rather than men! It is true to say that we did have an instructor leave his wife for a prisoner and also a very able Officer became involved with a young prisoner which regrettably led to the resignation of the former and the transfer of the latter. The issue of searching naturally arose, the male Officers were instructed to knock on the dormitory or room door before entering but it did, interestingly, raise the issue among some of the women who said they would prefer to be strip searched by a male Officer rather than an openly lesbian Officer - I was unable to resolve this one!

The policy that children should only be kept in the prison until they were 18 months old initially seemed to me to be harsh. However the majority of mums realized that their children were learning to talk, and they did not want them picking up the prison language e.g. "Where's the f...ing screw" etc., also the children needed to explore the great outdoors, including going shopping and travel on public transport etc. If the release date was only a month or two away we could be flexible. With sensible use of extra home leaves to acclimatise the child to whoever would be taking over care, only one or two mothers made an issue of the policy.

The Mother and Baby Unit was run by medically qualified nurses based in the unit at all times. Mothers mainly sat around all day watching the TV and with minimal interaction with their children and seemed to demonstrate a lack of knowledge of how to play with them. This seemed to me to be wrong for this was not what happened in the real world, what was needed was a thorough review. I took advice, and subsequently nursery nurses were hired; the number of medical staff was reduced and those remaining were transferred to a suitable building in the grounds. This also had the benefit of making all the women go to the "surgery", as they would in the community outside. A crèche was developed and mothers were given guidance on childcare and the skill which they seemed to be lacking of actually getting down and playing with the children. They were also able to attend education courses and other activities to develop themselves. The charity "Babies in Prison" gave great practical help as did the local Social Services, who helped break down the barrier of suspicion which many women felt towards social workers who they feared would be instrumental in removing their children from them. Indeed women who had committed acts of criminality did not necessarily mean they were uncaring or inadequate mothers.

Askham also held young prisoners, i.e. those under twenty-one years. From time to time questions arose as to whether this was appropriate, mixing all ages. In fact we found that the interaction between the age groups led to stability for older women who were able to absorb the frustrations of the younger group, and the younger never failed to inspire. When HQ made a proposal to take the under twenty-ones away we had tears and much anxiety from the youngsters, who saw transfer to a young prisoners' wing of a closed prison as a retrograde step. Similarly dormitories were said to restrict privacy, which indeed they did, but also provided the possibility of mutual support and comfort at stressful times. Mainly our half dozen or so Lifers coming to the end of their custody had single rooms, as did those who occupied the separate hostel from where they went out to work daily and, of course, Mothers with Babies.

The problem of "assertive" prisoners vexed me, for whilst staff were expected to assert themselves, they generally expected prisoners to be submissive. It always annoyed me when female staff and prisoners would apologise when there was simply no need to do so. It was expected that respect would be shown to staff by residents, a necessity in my book for order to be maintained, but it was also right that in return residents should be respected and given freedom where possible to express themselves. I felt that whilst we tried and had limited success, the problem of women who were, and always had been powerless and without any self-respect was a constant challenge in an inherently coercive environment. In truth it was in the Education and Probation Departments and in the various working parties with empathetic staff where much of this was able to progress and there were individual officers who rose to the occasion and worked one to one with individuals, understanding and accepting language and sometimes behavior which they understood as being the only way a woman knew to assert herself – such patience indeed. My oft-quoted comments were that "We will do nothing **for** you but will help you in every way to achieve for yourself." "Try to put aside being a victim; work toward being a survivor."

Staff themselves often ventured ideas and one novel suggestion came from an officer who volunteered to facilitate a Prisoner Consultative Committee, unusual in a prison setting. We discussed the rules, boundaries and election processes ensuring that representatives came from all categories of resident. Some lively meetings followed with a fair amount of "Can we have?" said with seductive reasoning and "No you can't", giving reasons why not, but also there were many positive outcomes. On one memorable occasion the issue was raised as to why all the women were required to get out of bed during the night for a roll call in the dining room, when a Night Patrol found a woman missing. This had been going on for years, and had it been in a prison for men I am sure that noisy and possibly violent protest would have taken place at a time when only three or four staff were on duty in the establishment. To my shame I had been in charge for some two or three years when this practice was raised. It was easy for staff to do a headcount without disturbing the whole community.

Derek Lewis became Director General and actually showed interest in women prisoner issues (as did his wife) as well as giving Governors more freedom to spend – and be accountable – for their budgets, hence our training trips. A few Governors of prisons for women were called to a meeting where we gave presentations, among which was the notorious form providing a male outline (for which there was no female version (why?)) on which bruises and body marks had to be recorded upon reception, to demonstrate that any injury had been inflicted prior to taking in the prisoner. He indicated to his Heads of Department that he wanted progress but alas events overtook him, and he was sacked by Michael Howard who had become Home Secretary, infamous for his statement that "Prison works". Periodically it seemed that acknowledgement was given to women's issues by an academic report or bad publicity, e.g. the shackling of women to beds during childbirth (apparently authorised by Ann Widdecombe, a Prisons Minister), and a fresh HQ appointment was made to indicate that "the Prison Service was taking action". Unfortunately these appointments, e.g. a female Chief Probation Officer on secondment, offered but temporary interest. This lack of awareness of male / female needs and practices by our hierarchy was demonstrated by an Area Manager, who demanded to know why we spent twice as much on toilet paper as another male establishment with twice our population. He failed to appreciate the uses to which women put toilet tissue but when asked about his wife and daughters usage accepted my explanation.

Absconding was not very common and with women it was usually a domestic worry, most often about a child's illness, which prompted the departure or occasionally shortly after arrival when they found the fact that they were not locked up difficult to come to terms with. Whilst men escaping could be anywhere, with women all the police had to do was to go to her home address which is where she would usually be found, the pull of their children irresistible. Overstaying home leaves were more common for women who would try to persuade GPs that they were unfit to travel etc etc etc.

We were, of course, not immune from tragedy. Our policy was to accommodate any prisoner offered to us if we could. One who came had a history of suicidal attempts and we took her on the basis that she appeared to be of more settled mind and that open conditions might benefit her. Unfortunately she was found in a WC cubicle where she had made serious cuts to her wrists. We had no full time medical cover and I decided that for her safety she should be immediately transferred to New Hall where such cover existed. She committed suicide there that night. At Askham staff were devastated and talking over among themselves whether they could have done something to prevent this, whether it had been right to transfer her, etc. I felt badly too, but this introspection by the staff became a blight on the running of the prison so I bluntly told the group when I found they had been closeted for an hour or more that if anyone was to blame, if that was what they were looking for, it had ultimately been my decision. We had a live resident population to consider.

There was always the conflict of the need of one individual and the need for the establishment as a unit to thrive. Occasionally this would mean that a prisoner would be the innocent party to feel the effect of this. A very able young officer was found to be meeting in a hotel with a young prisoner during what should have been the youngster's home-leave. When challenged the officer immediately resigned but given the feeling within the prison, among staff, I felt it best for the prisoner to be transferred. I had no doubt that the older officer was to blame and that the young person should not be penalized, nevertheless knowing the feelings of officers friendly to the one who had resigned I deemed it was better for her to have a fresh start elsewhere. Another well-regarded woman of mature years, a former nurse who had embezzled some money, left us and within a few days killed herself using a car exhaust. Some of us attended her funeral and her action appeared to be as much a mystery to her family as it was to us. It, perhaps, emphasized the point often made that prison is the easy part; it is the resettlement that is much harder. Her *Inside the Insider, Inside* observations begin this book.

One other sad event was the allegation brought against my male deputy by a woman we had transferred out. She waited until a couple of days before her actual release to claim that she had been raped by this Officer at Askham, and my deputy was suspended whilst the police investigated. The prisoners were supportive of him and claimed that the woman was not to be trusted, but due process had to be done. After what seemed an unnecessary delay the police notified us of the time and date of the offence; then we were able to demonstrate by documentation and witnesses of both Officer and prisoner that he had spent the whole period chairing a sentence planning board in another part of the prison. On his return I had the Fire Alarm (we regularly held surprise fire practices) sounded so that the whole community was able to welcome him. Unfortunately his wife insisted that he apply for a transfer back to a male prison.

Something which I felt strongly about was the discontinuance of transferring women to open conditions by car, who by virtue of their destination indicated that only minimum supervision was required. The cellular vehicles introduced by the private contractors, though suitable for transporting prisoners securely, had shortcomings when used in the Women's Estate. On long journeys with men, the availability of calling in to a prison en-route for a comfort break was there due to the number of prisons for men around the country. For women on the other hand they had to endure journeys lasting hours because of the few prisons into which they could call. It could have been arranged by the escort to call at police stations but this seemed beyond them. Because the driver and escort were simply deliverers of "goods" they paid no attention to the security status or comfort needs of the prisoner and therefore would not allow a woman coming to an open prison to use a motorway facility. Not only the fact that women had to suffer (often abusive) male prisoners in the same vehicle, to travel from Holloway to Askham takes some hours, and in claustrophobic confinement, usually without food or relief I regarded as barbaric, especially for those with allergies or dietary needs.

Another issue where my outdated chauvinistic views lost out was the issue of urine sampling. I tried to resist its introduction in Askham on grounds of dignity and privacy, because generally at that time drugs for us were not a major issue and with dormitory accommodation we pretty quickly learned of anyone taking or peddling drugs. With the benefit of hindsight and the current situation perhaps I was wrong.

Whilst attending an official reception aboard the *Sobriety*, a boat project in Goole where we sent women to assist helping handicapped passengers, I heard an author give a talk about how a book could be written in a day. This was Brian Lewis and during lunch I asked if he was interested in writing a book about Askham and this led to him writing *"The Story of a House"*[1] with help from myself, staff and prisoners. It won the Raymond Williams literary prize.

Passing a promotion board, I had to participate in the prison service Senior Management course run by Kings College, London and as part of that had to undertake a study of another country's prison service. Since the short period had to be taken during January or February I was fortunate to be one of a mixed disciplinary group selected to go to Uganda. Most of the other groups went off to Canada or countries in Europe where they suffered freezing temperatures, apparently tempered by copious amounts of alcohol. Our little group was able to add on some annual leave, paying our own way, and enjoyed wonderful hospitality from our hosts who took us, for which we contributed to the fuel costs, to every prison via a national park – or so it seemed. On one occasion, breaking down and spending the night in the van surrounded by wild animals - the men together got out to pee but our lone woman showed her mettle by holding on until morning!

Poverty was apparent everywhere and we certainly saw how to manage with humanity on minimal funding - often staff were not paid for some months, basics for maintenance were missing and prisoners could spend years awaiting trial. However the most significant thing from my perspective was that prisoners could take on tasks unsupervised and also, if considered suitable and trustworthy, were able to be employed by the prison after release.

At one prison for women, we were entertained by singing and dancing. I later suggested that our group might return with some fruit and formally thank them for their welcome. This we did. However the arrangement was formal, with us meant to sit at a table on a raised platform whilst the women, several with babies, sat on the floor. Not liking what struck me as "official and colonial" I joined the women on the floor, which seemed to be appreciated by them although one infant screamed aloud, apparently because he had never seen a white face before.

The hardship of the prisoners, both male and female, was serious, for whilst they had food (cooked over open fires in the prison courtyard), there was a shortage of beds and bedding. This lack of a blanket was because a family might only have one blanket between them and when one parent was sent to prison the other kept the blanket for the family. The poverty of the country meant that prisons supplied food but little else. Half the prize money Brian and I won for "ASKHAM - The Story of a House" was donated to the women prisoners in Uganda (the other half going to the charity "Women In Prison".)

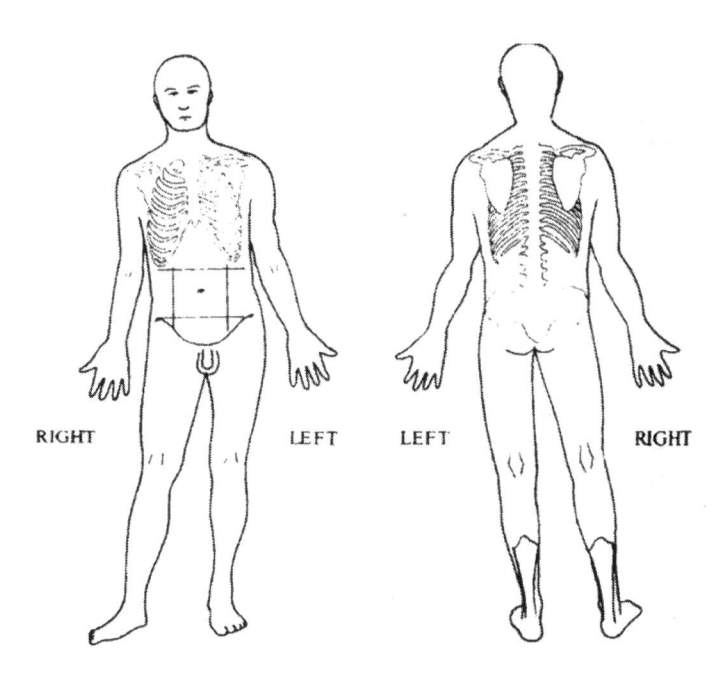

Form used on reception in both male <u>and female prisons</u> to show existing bodily marks and injuries

HRH Princess Anne's visit

Newspaper heading: Barking Mad Governor

7. The Barking Mad Governor

Although I had had some dealings with the media during my career, notably over a number of absconds from Lowdham Grange and the 50 year commemoration of the 1930 march previously mentioned, it was at Askham where I learned to "proactively manage" the local media, inviting reporters in and feeding positive stories to the likes of the *Yorkshire Evening Post,* so that when adverse news arose they would normally contact me for a view. This gave the opportunity to scotch any wild assertions. However I couldn't cover all eventualities ...

We had a woman prisoner allocated to us and she was deemed very unsettled, verging on becoming disruptive. A member of the Board of Visitors found that she had no family, and had been forced to leave her pet dog with a cousin; she was desperate for re-assurance that the dog was alright. The prisoner's view was that other women had children and partners visit, why could she not see her dog just once to reassure herself that it was okay. She assured me that it was well behaved so I agreed that the dog might be brought in and allowed to visit at a suitable time. The dog, a huge bull mastiff, arrived and was so excited to see her that it fouled the visits room (which the prisoner cleared up), they went on a walk around the grounds and the woman was transformed for the better. A mole within the prison reported this event to an MP and the *Yorkshire Evening Post* headlined "Barking Mad Governor".

A reporter from a Sunday paper managed unbeknown to ourselves to enter the prison during an open day charity fundraising event and persuaded a prisoner to meet him on her next town visit. They met, had tea in a café and departed. However as he entered his car and she went to walk away he called her back, she bent to the window and a photographer in the car behind took a picture. The ensuing article headlined "Porridge with Oats" in the

Sunday Mirror suggested that prisoners were indulging in prostitution. The unfortunate lass was mortified, and I had HQ in a panic. We challenged the paper and they agreed not to publish the name of the woman but chose to deny entrapment, although they did permit me to make a brief response. Naturally one had to recognize that a woman on parole could get up to many things including prostitution, but thankfully very few took advantage of trust placed in them. There was probably a wish not to spoil things for others also.

The headline "Killer wife hosts jail drinks bash" was earned from the Sunday Mirror which sensationalized a house blessing. Our Chaplain had negotiated a small terraced house for a "Lifer" who had been granted parole and was about to be released. She had asked him to bless her future home and he obviously agreed. She wished to provide for some simple refreshment for those who attended, and our Catering Officer agreed to do this in his own time on his rest day. I was invited together with some staff, members of the Board of Visitors and some of her friends, who were eligible for temporary release. Our resident "mole", whether for payment or sheer vindictiveness notified the Mirror - hence the headline with a story much embellished.

Reporters and photographers congregated outside the prison from very early in the morning because a notorious prisoner was to be released. However we had arranged for this woman to leave by the back garden exit to avoid a melee by the main entrance. A woman prisoner in an upstairs dormitory at the front of the house decided to bare her breasts at the window. This was not – to my knowledge - a deliberate ploy to divert attention from the infamous one being let out the back way, but simply exhibitionism, which led to a picture of the woman in the window appearing in the "*News of the World*" and the headline "A Prison Bust Out".

My visit to Uganda led to another criticism in the local media, this time by an MP from a neighbouring constituency who accused the Prison Service of sending me on a "jolly"; this I found amusing considering the number of overseas visits MPs made at public expense.

Woollen Penguin knitted by a prisoner at Askham Grange who was doing a relatively short sentence for being "a neighbour from hell" according to a northern newspaper. She reluctantly accepted the force of authority but refused to engage with ourselves, its' representatives. After several weeks of the overtures of one officer who refused to be put off by her "anti" attitude, she began to let the person underneath the hard exterior show. Subsequently she began to relate to some other staff and on her release presented me with this woolly toy, admitting that some people in authority were also human. She declined, however, to say where she had "found" the HMP uniform badge which adorned the penguin!

8. Reflections

Circumstances never did allow me to take up my promotion and so it all came to an end in 2000 for it was mandatory at the time to retire at 60 years of age. It was in fact a good time to go. Michael Howard had become Home Secretary in 1996 and politicized the treatment of prisoners more so than any predecessor. From then on successive governments tried to outdo each other in "making prison work", locking up more and more people whilst continually reducing the requisite resources and funding. Those in charge had become functionaries and had, I was sure, become geared to knowing the cost of everything and the value of nothing; it was no longer the Prison Service which had had the vibrancy of spirit which had enthused and led me to join, indeed I had passed my "sell by date".

The strength of the English Prison System had always been the relationship between the prisoner and Officer. I felt the movement to management by HQ edict was dis-empowering Governors, and that allowing profit to be gained from the incarceration of the state's citizens by privatization had initiated the race to the bottom: reductions in staffing levels and resourcing meant the lessons of the costly riots of 1986 and early 1990s were again being forgotten. Towards the end of my time in charge prison officers were removed from running the prison shop where prisoners had always been able to spend their earnings enabling the officer to keep a check on individuals spending, watching for any bullying and offering advice on budgeting as well as getting the best prices at the wholesalers for the goods stocked. When this became a privatised pre-ordering system prices rocketed and quality went down which mattered when earnings were only £3 or £4 per week every penny mattered.

The prison Education Department and operation of the Library were contracted out to Education providers sometimes based 100 miles away and the transport of prisoners was privatised. Catering likewise went which often led to sandwiches or packaged food instead of a hot meal. I understand that after I left the Works Department went the same way. Hence Governors did less governing and became Contract Managers.

When I started there was a great debate over the purpose of imprisonment – and it still goes on, especially when conditions deteriorate and it reaches public consciousness. There are indeed a significant number of people who are a continuing danger to society, but the vast majority of prisoners want to get through their sentence with minimum trouble, and many can and do improve themselves if given opportunity. All along I have felt that without having the resources and the ability to stimulate a desire to change, incarceration, apart from a period of public protection, becomes frustrating and often a complete waste of time. It is in fact after release that the real punishment starts for many, if not most. Prisoners have lost their job (if they had one), their home and often their relationship with partner and family. To rebuild these in the face of continued branding as "an Ex-Prisoner" is no easy matter and requires bravery and resilience. Experience and common sense tells us that to enable prisoners to learn, to change and on release to be encouraged and supported is, for the majority and especially for young offenders, the best crime prevention strategy to benefit society – if only the money were redirected. To quote Mary Size from 1952: "We must remember that inmates of penal establishments will return to the community sooner or later, and will sit beside us in the train, on the bus, at the films, or in the restaurant, with no bars between and no walls round them. Unless we have planted the seeds of self- respect, moral integrity, and a desire to become an asset instead of a liability to the State, we have not protected society from the criminal and we have failed in our mission." Unfortunately it often seems we have learned nothing for there is an articulate element in society who wish to punish, and punish harshly, without redemption, despite the financial and human cost, and unfortunately politicians are only exercised when something sensational occurs, for there have never been votes in prison.

The primary purpose of a prison is to keep in custody those committed by the Courts and therefore security has to be the focus. However security not only involves physical containment but also emotional and psychological aspects, hence safety and welfare and engagement must be addressed. Control of the environment by staff is essential for safety both for themselves and for prisoners alike. Staff who feel insecure lose confidence and this is quickly picked up by prisoners who themselves then feel at risk of bullying and intimidation. Fortunately most prison staff wish to see the protection of the public as more than just containment, hence it has long been recognized that constructive use of the time by individual development, education, practical training and dealing where possible with identifiable need gives some hope that the prisoner will not turn to crime in future.

Do I regret my time? No, I am pleased to have answered the advertisement which stated "Management with a Social Purpose" and participated at a time when there was a tacit agreement between Home Secretaries of whatever hue that the Prison Service was a Public Service and that Governors were given wide discretion and expected to lead as well as manage their prisons. It was an interesting and varied career during which I met a whole range of people, saw the best and the worst of behaviours (the Christian adage about "Hate the sin but Love the Sinner" comes to mind) but also gained great satisfaction, most particularly at Askham Grange. I have often been asked if I "enjoyed" my work to which my response is that no-one should be in the job who "enjoys" locking other people up – it is a necessity which is part of the work.

I believe governing is about leadership, management and teamwork. My experiences demonstrated that at some establishments there were good leaders but weak managers or sometimes any combination of the three elements which were not always in kilter. I am not claiming to have succeeded in all three areas but I did my best to keep a balance of the three in mind. One of the downsides of a disciplined service like the Prison Service is that Governors have little control over personnel who are posted in, and all know of staff in whom he/she has little confidence and who can be destructive if of a mind. Yet on the whole, if a firm statement of direction of travel is communicated from the top, the majority will follow and what is more, if listened to, will gladly contribute. My time with the Inspectorate interviewing staff at various prisons showed that they knew the failures and often the corrections to be made without any need on my part to come up with magic solutions. Individuals would talk of "following a particular superior officer through fire" and I served with those about whom I felt the same. Liking is not the same as respect and difficult decisions have to be taken: telling someone that their job is no longer viable, that a prisoner has to be transferred for no other reason than that an improper relationship existed with a member of staff (who resigned), or that external blanket directives imposed changes which seem perverse. The conflict between the individual, be they prisoner or staff, and the needs of the institution, is ever present.

There remains always the institutional drift towards operating in favour of staff convenience, i.e. the powerful body of discipline Officers who naturally wish to keep social hours themselves. Hence the lunchtime meal was served in most prisons at 11.30 am because Officers wished to have their meal at midday. This tendency applied to most activities even to the extent sometimes of denying prisoners their daily exercise because "it looked like rain". Many would say that as prisoners they should not complain and indeed they did not, but it could and did inhibit the making of real life experience of work and education periods. The need to balance the regime to respect the contribution of all departments was not always easy to achieve. In some quarters, and I heard it expressed by officers from time to time, "Happiness is door shaped". An officer promoted to Senior Officer arrived at Lowdham Grange but after a few days asked to revert to his former prison because "he could not stand having the trainees around him all the time".

Finally the overall feeling I have is that my whole career equipped and led me to the Governorship of Askham Grange. The combination of all those postings and events along the way I believe enabled me to direct its development at a challenging time, and to give staff trust and confidence in themselves from which to encourage those women sent to us to see the possibility of hope for the future. So the key question everyone should ask themselves often during their career, and especially at the end, is: "Did I make a difference?" With the help of many others I tried often and sometimes did. Certainly the number of letters and cards we received from prisoners who had successfully resettled helps me to believe it.

ACKNOWLEDGEMENTS

First I must express my appreciation to my successive deputy governors and the officers at Askham Grange who supported me during my time in charge. All departments of the prison contributed to the goals of the whole enterprise but of special note were Education and Probation led by remarkable people whose drive and commitment to changing the women's perception of themselves to be people of worth able to grow self confidence and achieve their own targets during their time in custody and hopefully after release.

All magnificently rose to the challenge to turn Askham into a prison which consistently achieved remarkable results for the successful resettlement of women into society after their imprisonment and I cannot praise them too much.

For the encouragement throughout to actually get this book into print my thanks to Brian Lewis. His ideas, his reviewing the progress and imposing necessary discipline at times has always been done with charm and humour.

To Alison Dempster whose patience with proof reading and editing successive drafts has been tested to the full. Thank you,

I am indebted to Ang Lewis for photographic help.

My son Anthony gave me much help with the mysteries of my computer as did Sue Smith.

To proof readers / commentators Debbie Hodgson, Julia Woodhall, Lesley and John Taylor I am indebted.

Finally, John Young of eebygumbooks came to my rescue by lifting all the stress of design and printing arrangements from my shoulders. What seemed an insurmountable problem to me he simply took over. So a yard or two of ale whenever convenient John!

APPENDICES

Appendix 1

Matthew 25:34-40 New International Version (NIV)

34 "Then the King will say to those on his right, 'Come, you who are blessed by my Father; take your inheritance, the kingdom prepared for you since the creation of the world. <u>35 For I was hungry and you gave me something to eat, I was thirsty and you gave me something to drink, I was a stranger and you invited me in, 36 I needed clothes and you clothed me, I was sick and you looked after me, I was in prison and you came to visit me.'</u>

37 "Then the righteous will answer him, 'Lord, when did we see you hungry and feed you, or thirsty and give you something to drink? 38 When did we see you a stranger and invite you in or needing clothes and clothe you? 39 When did we see you sick or in prison and go to visit you?'

40 "The King will reply, 'Truly I tell you, whatever you did for one of the least of these brothers and sisters of mine, you did for me.'

This sentence underlined seemed very important to my idealistic thinking of the time and this poem by Leigh Hunt "Abou Ben Adhem" also spoke to me:

Appendix 2

Abou Ben Adhem - Leigh Hunt

Abou Ben Adhem (may his tribe increase!)
Awoke one night from a deep dream of peace,
And saw, within the moonlight in his room,
Making it rich, and like a lily in bloom,
An angel writing in a book of gold:—
Exceeding peace had made Ben Adhem bold,
And to the presence in the room he said,
"What writest thou?"—The vision raised its head,
And with a look made of all sweet accord,
Answered "The names of those who love the Lord."
"And is mine one?" said Abou. "Nay, not so,"
Replied the angel. Abou spoke more low,
But cheerly still; and said, "I pray thee, then,
Write me as one that loves his fellow men."

The angel wrote, and vanished. The next night
It came again with a great wakening light,
And showed the names whom love of God had blest,
And lo! Ben Adhem's name led all the rest.

Appendix 3

One of our prisoners who had been sentenced for murder at the age of 15 years in a teenage gang melee wrote the following:

MYSELF
I have to live with myself and so
I want to be fit for myself to know.
I want to be able as days go by
Always to look myself straight in the eye
I don't want to stand in the setting sun
and hate myself for the things I've done.

I don't want to keep on a closet shelf
a lot of secrets about myself.
And feel myself as I come and go
into thinking that no-one else will know
the kind of person I really am.
I don't want to dress myself in a sham.

I can never hide myself from me,
I see what others may never see.
I know what others may never know.
I can never fool myself and so
whatever happens I want to be
self-respecting and conscience free.

Appendix 4

The following was written by one of our Probation Team which I found a joy to read for it expressed much of our humour of the time.

The Overpopulated Prison (with apologies to Oliver Goldsmith)

Part 1

Sweet Askham fairest prison in the vale
more like a health farm than a normal jail,
where Harry and his disparate crew
strive to organise this human zoo

Where Barney sniffs through every glade
and furtive dealers ply their ancient trade.
Where wanton women hawk their well used wares
and pimps recruit their molls at Christmas fairs

See the phallic tower rise
thrusting up towards the skies,
symbol of this den of sin,
herald of what lies within.

For in this place whence all wise men have fled
the convicts often sleep two in a bed.
Oh trysts of lust sublime!
Oh beds of concupiscence divine
'tis strange how a prison can also be
a hall of carnal liberty.

The centre of this viper's nest
jumps and scurries at the telephone's behest.
Here nerves are taut and tempers frayed
and vital papers often get mislaid.

See the whining convict at the stable door,
hear the plangent voice implore
For news of her recent petition
to go home with the utmost expedition.

The answer's "No!" which doesn't satisfy
and the prisoner begins to shout and cry.
With this, the S.O.'s nerves unravel
and he starts to counsel her on sex and travel.

With flowing tears for all to see
she finds a member of the BOV.
This fine body is good at doing good
And her sad plight is quickly understood.
G.V's, Probation and Chaplain courted
the original order is soon aborted.
Her problem solved, our happy rover
hurries home for a quick leg-over.

There stands Grange Row, seat of therapy benign,
where whinging convicts seek to exculpate their crime.
Here groups are led and heads are shrunk
and torpid brains get filled with bunk.
And, as if to condone their sin
John Taylor hands out biscuits from a tin.

The admin staff sweat blood all day
to try and keep the bumpf at bay
with eyes gone square from screens that glow
and brains gone numb from working so.

But never fear, they'll soon be sold
to a consortium, for a crock of gold,
For all the while, the goalposts caper
across a field whose turf is paper.

Part 2

But, 'tis easy for the bard to mock
to raise a smirk, and try to shock.
Better to forswear such bile
and laud the virtues of this stately pile.

At Askham, a priceless gem we own -
A "civil society" as once was known
'ere the Thatcher Witch assumed the throne
or grey King John began to drone.

The weak are succoured, not turned away
and Jungle Law is kept at bay.
Skills are encouraged and confidence enhanced;
problems tackled and hope advanced.

To prepare for freedom is our aim
not some unctuous politician's game.
For, if self-control is to awaken
some risks must perforce be taken.
The occasional scandal makes The Sun
and lodges there 'twixt tit and bum.
For failure is what the tabloids want to hear
it makes the readers hate and fear.

But the unrecorded and unsung gains
Far outweigh the infrequent pains.
Better to try and sometimes fail
than pander to the Daily Mail.

The staff don't toil for Group 4's tawdry gold
But for a public service not yet sold.
"Downsized", pushed and messed about
they often want to scream and shout

Yet though staff be worn down to the bone,
no weeping prisoner is left to cry alone;
humanity and help hold sway,
'ere "market forces" come into play.

Such help can at times extend
right down to a canine friend,
Even though it raise a frown
we'll go as far as Chapeltown!

If it sometimes veers towards insanity,
what is that against humanity?
So here's to Harry and his noble ship
and for Michael Howard a bowl of s**t.

© J.Taylor 1997. Former Probation Officer at Askham Grange.
"Reproduction in any form without permission will result in strenuous and vindictive litigation".

Appendix 5

LESSONS in LIVING – for my grandchildren:

- give and work to get a smile; be kind.
- put brain into gear before opening mouth;
- give respect and try not to make unthinking judgments or assumptions;
- am I making a difference?
- integrity is doing the right thing even if it not convenient;
- the best job is the one you would do even if you didn't have to;
- give advice only when asked BUT do not expect it to be taken;
- if you can say nothing good then say nothing (or at least be factual!);
- have PATIENCE and LISTEN (actively to what is being said);
- delay is better than disaster.

References

The Story of a House – Askham Grange Women's Open Prison; Edited by Brian Lewis and Harry Crew, Forward by Helena Kennedy QC, Yorkshire Art Circus in association with Askham Grange / HM Prison Service 1997   ISBN 1-898311-30-7

Prisons I Have Known. Mary Size; George Allen & Unwin Ltd 1957

When The Gates Shut. Joanna Kelley MA,LLD, FSA ; Longmans,Green and Co Ltd. 1967

The Better Fight.   The Story of Dame Lilian Barker. Elizabeth Gore; Geoffrey Bles 1965

Family Documents:

List of the Name Crew taken from the
Bindings of the Company of Watermen & Lightermen of the River Thames

Boys Name		Commenced	Place	Master		Freedom	Ref
Crew	Alexander	7/11/1746	Bermondey	Selby	Jacob	15/2/1754	786
Crew	Samual	17/8/1770	Bermondeay	Crew	Alexander	18/9/1777	775
Crew	Jno	14/3/1782	Bermondsey	Crew	Alexander #	16/4/1789	774
Crew	Samual Thomas	24/7/1800	Bermondsey	Crew	John	28/8/1817	751
Crew	John	25/1/1810	Bermondsey	Crew	John	8/5/1817	736
Crew	William	13/5/1830	Wandsworth	Constable	Charles	13/7/1837	738
Crew	Samual Thomas	14/2/1833	Rotherhithe	Crew	Samual Thomas	9/4/1840	737
Crew	John Jnr	12/11/1840	St Mary's at Hill	Crew	John Snr	9/8/1849	721
Crew	Charles	13/7/1854	Wandsworth	Crew	William	10/6/1862	741
Crew	William Hanley	9/4/1857	Wandsworth	King	George	10/4/1866	742
Crew	John Danial	11/5/1869	Whitechapel	Crew	John	8/6/1875	719
Crew	John William Thomas	13/6/1893	Bermondsey	Crew	John Danial	9/10/1900	1354
Crew	Percy	13/8/1895	Greenwich	Allen	William Thomas	Drowned	1355

Bindings of the Company of Watermen and Lightermen of the River Thames listing the CREW name.

Great Grandfather John Daniel Crew

DEATH OF A WELL-KNOWN WATERMAN.

South Bermondsey loses a well-known character in the person of the late John Daniel Crew, who passed away on December 24th. Mr. Crew was a Thames waterman for over 50 years, and was generally occupied taking buyers out to the Dutch eel boats which lay up in the river near London Bridge. There was a cessation of this trade when war broke out in 1914, and Mr. Crew, who was so used to this traffic, ceased work, never to resume it. In spite of the arduous life he had led, Mr. Crew lived to the good age of 78 years.

The interment took place on Tuesday at Nunhead Cemetery, and was witnessed by many old friends.

Obituary of John Daniel Crew, my Great Grandfather

Grandfather John William Thomas Crew

Grandmother Ada Florence Crew

**Grandfather and Grandmother Crew
in later life**

Grandfather Mitchell

My mother enjoying rowing

Father Henry (Harry) H Crew

Grandfather Mitchell with my mother Hilda before their flight to France c.1930

Mother in a reflective mood

Dad's Fish Stall, 1930's

My parents' wedding, 1937

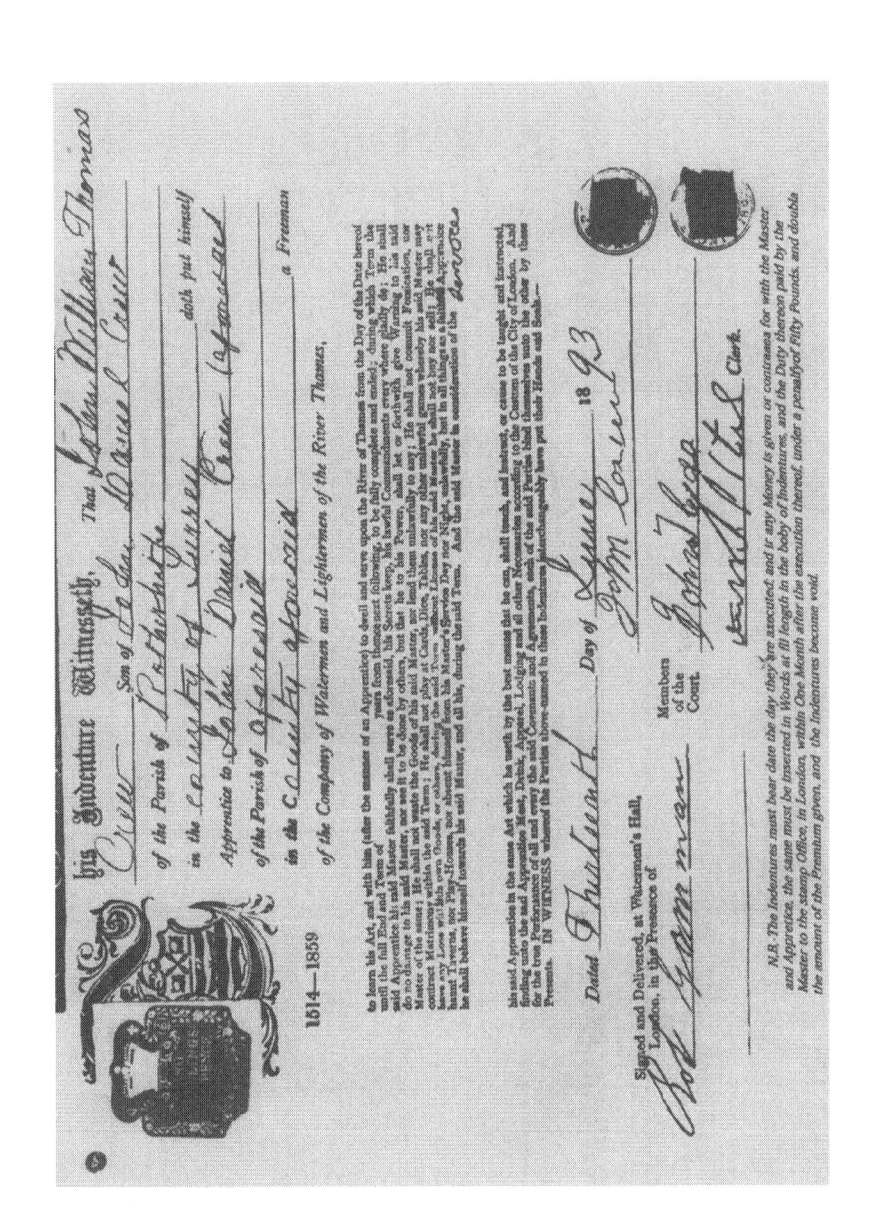

Apprentice Waterman's Bindings

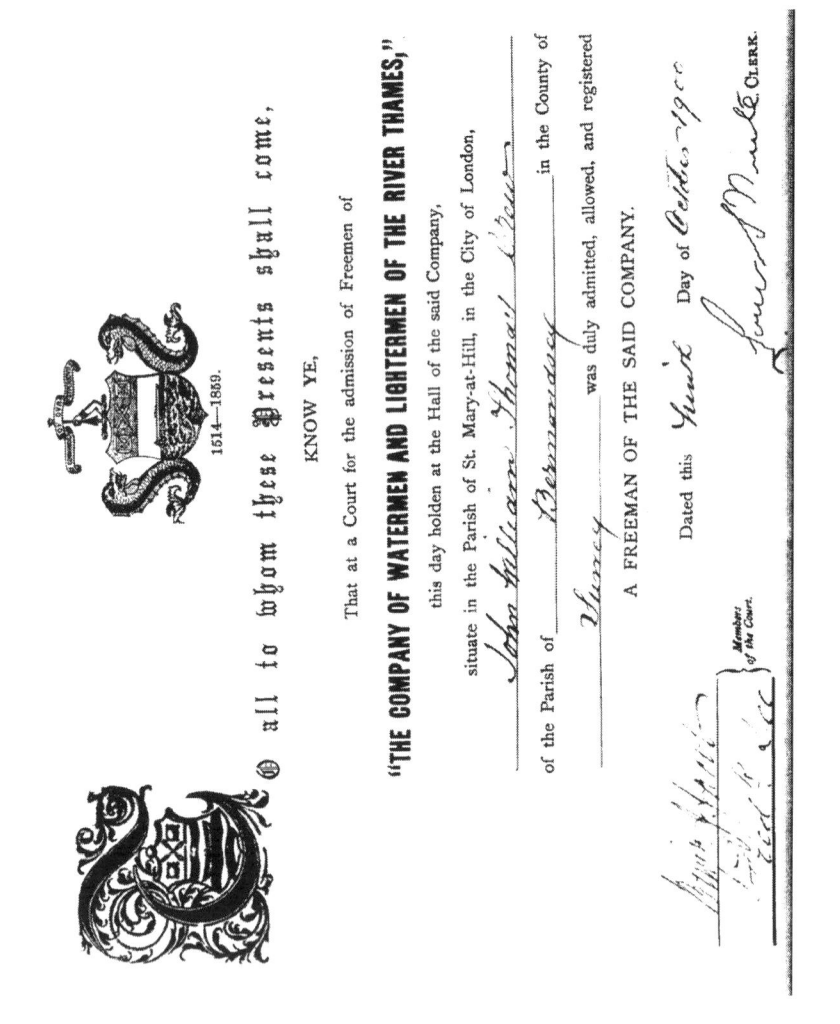

**Admission to Freeman of the River Thames.
Granted on completion of apprenticeship.**

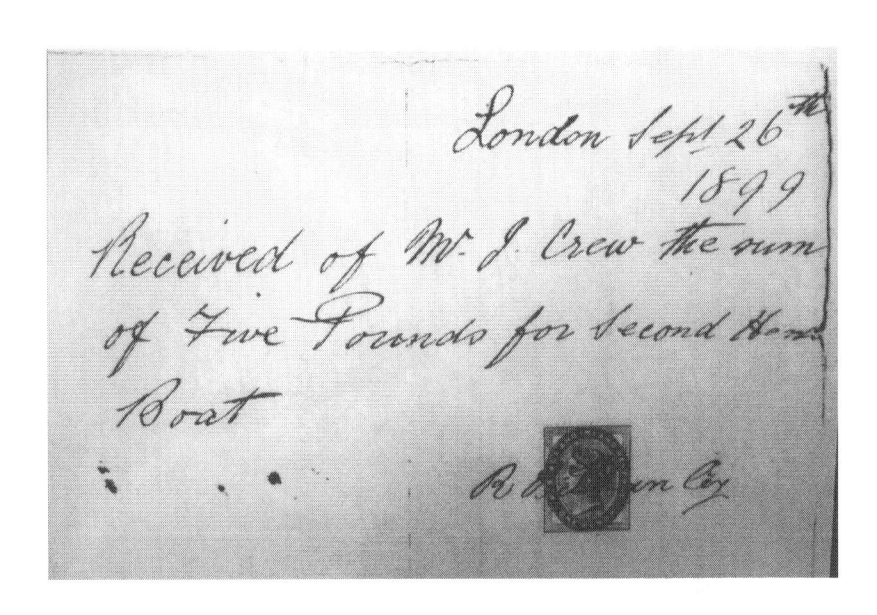

Boat Purchase Receipt

BILLINGSGATE MARKET.

This LICENCE must be delivered up upon the expiration thereof, with the Badge given therewith, to the Clerk of the Market:— If required to be renewed, the Licence must be deposited at the Clerk's Office for that purpose on the first Monday in June of each year.

Nº. 468

PORTER'S LICENCE.

THE MARKETS COMMITTEE, appointed by the Corporation of the City of London, to execute the power to grant Licences to Porters, conferred by the Bye-Laws duly made for the regulation of Billingsgate Market, do hereby License

John William T. Grew

of 5 Colina Road

St. Bermondsey

to act as Porter within the said Market, and to stand and ply for hire therein accordingly.

This Licence is to continue in force until the first day of July, One thousand Nine hundred _____ provided the said _____ shall abide by the Bye-Laws, Rules, Orders, and Regulations which have been or may hereafter be duly made and approved for the Market; but if and in case the said _____ shall at any time hereafter be guilty of dishonesty or drunkenness, or do any other act which, in the opinion of the Markets Committee, shall be in violation of either of such Bye-Laws, Rules, Orders and Regulations, then and in every such case the said Committee shall be entitled, at their pleasure, to suspend or revoke this Licence; and from and immediately afterwards a Notice in writing of such suspension or revocation shall be signed by the Clerk of the Market, and shall be handed to the said _____ or transmitted to him through the Post, directed to his last known place of abode; and within Twenty-four hours after the said Notice shall have been so transmitted, the power and authority of the said _____ to act as a Porter shall entirely cease and determine, and if he shall so act thereafter, he shall be liable to the penalties for acting without a Licence, unless and until the said Committee shall grant another Licence to him, or shall, by a Note in writing at the back hereof, remove such suspension, and authorize him to act again as a Porter for the remainder of the year.

By Order of the Committee.

Billingsgate Fish Market Porters Licence.

Printed in Great Britain
by Amazon